직독직해로 읽는
오헨리 단편선
O. Henry's Short Stories

직독직해로 읽는
오헨리 단편선
O. Henry's Short Stories

개정판 2쇄 발행 2020년 6월 30일
초판 1쇄 발행   2011년 1월 10일

원작 오헨리
역주 이현구, 홍명표, 박기윤
디자인 IndigoBlue
일러스트 정은수
발행인 조경아
발행처 랭귀지북스
주소 서울시 마포구 포은로2나길 31 벨라비스타 208호
전화 02.406.0047   **팩스** 02.406.0042
이메일 languagebooks@hanmail.net
홈페이지 www.languagebooks.co.kr
등록번호 101-90-85278   **등록일자** 2008년 7월 10일
ISBN 979-11-5635-054-5 (13740)
가격 12,000원
ⓒ LanguageBooks 2011
잘못된 책은 구입한 서점에서 바꿔 드립니다.
blog.naver.com/languagebook에서 MP3 파일을 다운로드할 수 있습니다.

이 도서의 국립중앙도서관 출판예정도서목록(CIP)은 서지정보유통지원시스템 홈페이지(http://seoji.nl.go.kr)와
국가자료공동목록시스템(http://www.nl.go.kr/kolisnet)에서 이용하실 수 있습니다. (CIP제어번호 : CIP2016028788)

직독직해로 읽는
오헨리 단편선
O. Henry's Short Stories

오헨리 원작
이현구 역주

Language Books

머리말

　요즈음 영어 교육의 열기는 굳이 설명하지 않아도 누구나 알 것입니다. 수많은 학습자들은 자신에게 어울리는 공부법을 찾기 위해 학원을 다니고, 학습서로 공부해보지만, 좋은 공부법을 찾기란 쉽지 않은 일입니다.

　이런 분들이 영어 실력을 효율적으로 기르는 방법으론 원서를 읽으며 공부하는 것이 있습니다. 원서로 읽기 능력을 키우고, 어휘력과 표현력을 신장하여 여러 시험에 필요한 영어 실력을 효과적으로 준비할 수 있습니다. 그러나 원어민들이 즐겨 읽는 원서나 고전 작품에는 어려운 어휘와 표현이 많다는 단점이 있습니다.

　이렇게 자신에게 맞는 공부법을 찾는 데 어려움을 겪고 있는 분들과, 높은 수준의 원서를 혼자 공부하기 힘들어하는 분들을 위해 이 책을 쓰게 되었습니다. 다시 말하여 영어 학습에 도움이 될 만한 작품들을 여러분이 쉽게 이해할 수 있도록 직독직해로 설명해 놓았습니다. 게다가 원작의 내용을 이해하는데 아무런 문제가 없도록 글의·구성에 정성을 기울였습니다. 직독직해로 설명하는 목적은 직독직해로 읽는 습관을 익히면, 읽기 속도를 모국어 수준으로 높일 수 있기 때문입니다.

PREFACE

　또한 본 교재로 듣기와 말하기를 연습할 수 있도록, 원어민 성우가 녹음한 MP3 파일을 다운로드 할 수 있게 구성하였습니다. 직독직해로 해설해놓은 작품에는 대화체 표현이 많기 때문에, 회화에 필요한 수많은 표현을 익힐 수 있습니다.

　거기다 수능을 준비하는 학생들을 위하여 원서의 난이도를 조정했습니다. 실제로 본 책에서 설명된 대부분의 어휘들은 수능 수준의 어휘에 속합니다. 또한 문법, 숙어 표현, 회화 표현, 작가의 독특한 표현들을 설명하여 독자가 공부하는데 어려움이 없도록 하였습니다.

　분명 영어를 공부하는 것은 힘든 과정이지만, 유창하고 높은 수준의 영어를 자유자재로 사용할 수 있으려면, 영어를 장기간 공부해야 됩니다. 그 시간을 최대한 단축시키기 위해 저는 이 책을 쓰게 된 것입니다. 하지만 가장 중요한 것은 학습자의 마음가짐입니다. 부디 이 책과 여러분의 성실함을 무기로 큰 성과를 올리길 기대해 봅니다.

　본 책이 출판되도록 큰 도움을 주신 Language Books 사장님께 감사드립니다. 그리고 원고 준비과정에 도움을 준 제자 이현탁에게 감사의 뜻을 전합니다.

이현구

저자 소개

저자 오헨리에 대해서

O. Henry(1862-1910)

오헨리는 미국의 소설가로 미국 노스캐롤라이나에서 태어났다. 본명은 윌리엄 시드니 포터(William Sydney Porter)이다.

어린 시절 양친을 잃고 여러 직업을 전전하며 어렵게 생활했다. 노스캐롤라이나에서 유년기를 보냈고 텍사스에서 사춘기와 청년기를 보냈다.

1879년 고등학교를 졸업하고 삼촌이 경영하는 약국의 조수로 들어가 약사 자격증을 취득했다. 1889년 첫 작품을 발표했으나 그다지 큰 반응은 얻지 못했다.

오하이오 주에서는 오헨리가 다니던 은행에서 계산 실수를 했다는 이유로 고소를 당하여 오하이오 교도소에 수감되었다. 오헨리는 3년간 복역하면서 자신의 경험을 토대로 단편소설을 쓰기 시작했다.

INTRODUCTION

    오헨리라는 필명에 대한 유래에는 여러 가지 설이 있다. 텍사스 주 오스틴에서 살 때 길 잃은 가족 고양이를 "오! 헨리"라고 부르고 다닌 데서 유래했다는 설도 있고 오하이오 교도소의 교도소장 오린 헨리에서 영감을 얻었다는 설도 있다.

    아무튼 '오헨리'라는 필명으로 출간한 작품이 널리 알려지게 되면서 윌리엄 시드니 포터는 오헨리라는 이름으로 알려졌다.

    오헨리는 마감일에 편집자들의 눈에 띄지 않게 숨어버리기로 유명한 신문기자이기도 했다. 〈뉴욕 월드 썬데이 매거진〉이라는 잡지에 단편 381편을 실었다.

    오헨리의 작품은 주로 미국 남부나 뉴욕 뒷골목에 사는 가난한 서민과 빈민들의 애환을 그려 내었다. 그의 작품의 특징은 기발한 착상과 단순한 캐릭터, 쉬운 내러티브, 유머, 절묘한 구성이 특징이다. 특히 뜻밖의 결말이 독자들의 흥미를 돋운다.

    오헨리는 체호프, 모파상과 함께 세계 3대 단편소설 작가로 불린다.

직독직해 가이드

직독직해로 읽어야 영어소설을 감각적으로 즐길 수 있다.

　직독직해로 영어를 빠르게 이해하려면, 영어 문장의 순서에 따라 앞에 있는 말과 다음에 나오는 말과 어떤 관계인지 자연스럽게 느낄 수 있어야 합니다. 즉 영어의 어순대로 문장의 의미를 파악하는 훈련을 해야 합니다. 게다가 직독직해로 영어를 이해하려면, 문장구조를 파악하면서 기본 문법 지식을 활용해야 합니다.

　하지만 길고 복잡한 문장을 이해할 때, 더 많은 문법 지식이 필요한 것은 아닙니다. 이런 문장을 쉽게 이해하는 방법은 매우 간단합니다. 그것은 어려운 문법을 따져가며 문장을 분석하기보다 영어의 언어 논리를 익히는 것입니다.

　아래에 있는 문장은 "마지막 잎새"에 나옵니다. 직독직해에 익숙하지 않은 사람이라면, 영어 문장을 앞뒤로 읽으며 해석합니다.

<u>In one corner</u> <u>was</u> <u>a blank canvas</u> <u>on an easel</u>
　　　1　　　　　2　　　　3　　　　　　4

<u>that had been waiting there for twenty-five years</u> <u>to receive</u>
　　　　　　　　　　　5　　　　　　　　　　　　　　　　　6

<u>the first line of the masterpiece</u>.
　　　　　　　7

GUIDE

앞에 있는 문장을 우리말 어순에 따라 해석하면, 다음과 같습니다.

한쪽 구석에는(1) / 아무 그림도 없는 캔버스가(3) / 이젤 위에(4) / 있었는데(2) / 명작의 첫 번째 대열에 속한다는(7) / 대우를 받으려고(6) / 25년 동안 거기에 있었던 것이다.(5)

다시 말하여 영어 문장은 1-2-3-4-5-6-7 순서이지만, 우리말 어순에 맞게 해석해보면, 1-3-4-2-7-6-5 순으로 이해할 수 있습니다. 이런 순서로 이해하려면, 한 문장을 이해하는데 많은 시간이 걸립니다. 이런 방식으로 읽기를 지속하면, 긴 문장을 듣자마자 이해하는 것은 매우 어렵습니다. 또한 회화와 영작을 할 때, 영어로 유창하게 표현하는 능력이 개발되지 않습니다.

같은 문장을 영어 어순대로 이해하려면, 직독직해로 문장을 이해해야 합니다. 아래에 있는 설명처럼 이해할 수 있습니다.

In one corner → 한쪽 구석에는
was → 있었다.
a blank canvas → (무엇이 있었는가?) 아무 그림도 없는 캔버스가
on an easel → (캔버스는 어디에 있는가?) 이젤 위에
that had been waiting there for twenty-five years →
(그 그림 없는 캔버스는 어떤 것일까?) 25년 동안 거기에 있었던
to receive → (왜 기다리고 있었을까?) 대우를 받으려고
the first line of the masterpiece. → (어떤 대우를 받으려고 기다리는가?) 명작의 첫 번째 대열에 속한다는

앞의 설명에서 알 수 있듯이 영어는 우리말과 어순이 매우 다릅니다. 그래서 영어 어순대로 이해하는 연습을 해야 합니다. 이것이 직독직해를 익히는 첫 번째 단계일 뿐입니다. 그리고 앞에 나오는 단어나 표현을 보면, 다음에 어떤 내용이 올지 예측할 수 있는 힌트가 있습니다. 예를 들어 위의 문장을 보면, "was"라는 "be"동사가 "~이 있다, 존재하다"라는 의미로 쓰였습니다. "존재하다"라는 의미로 쓰인 "was"를 보자마자 "어떤 물건"이 "어디에" 있는지 예측할 수 있어야 합니다. 그래서 문장의 의미가 연결되는 힌트를 감각적으로 알아보려면, 영어의 언어논리를 익혀야 합니다.

영어의 논리를 쉽게 익히려면,

첫째, 주어, 동사, 목적어, 보어를 보고, 문장의 핵심 내용을 감각적으로 파악해야 합니다.

둘째, 동사의 종류에 따라 다음에 어떤 내용이 올지 예측할 수 있어야 합니다. 그래서 다양한 동사의 쓰임새에 익숙해져야 합니다.

셋째, 보통 관계 대명사나 부정사 앞에 나오는 내용을 보면, 다음에 어떤 내용이 올지 예측할 수 있어야 합니다. 즉 부정사와 관계대명사는 상황을 더 자세히 설명합니다.

넷째, 접속사를 보면서, 글에 나타나는 논리관계를 이해할 수 있어야 합니다.

다섯째, 대명사와 같은 기초 문법을 활용할 줄 알아야 합니다.

마지막으로 문법 학습에 지나치게 얽매이지 않도록 주의해야 합니다.

영어 문장을 읽자마자 이해하는 습관이 형성하면, 더 빠르게 읽고 이해할 수 있습니다. 이런 훈련을 하면, 스토리를 듣자마자 이해할 수 있습니다. 마지막 단계로 입으로 영작하는 연습을 게을리 하지 않습니다. 입으로 영어 문장을 유창하게 구사할 수 있다면, 회화와 영작이 즐거워집니다. 이런 입체적인 방법으로 공부하면, 원서를 읽고, 회화를 하는 것은 즐겁고 신나는 일이 됩니다.

읽기 가이드

『오헨리 단편선』을 읽으면서 최대 효과를 낼 수 있는 공부방법이 있습니다. 그것은 읽기 능력을 토대로, 듣기 연습을 하고, 듣기 능력을 토대로, 말하기 연습까지 하는 것입니다.

첫째, 직독직해로 읽는 연습을 하여, 원어민 속도로 읽는 것입니다.
둘째, 듣기 연습을 하여, 원어민이 빠르게 말하는 것을 듣고 이해하는 것입니다.
셋째, 동시통역 연습을 하여, 유창하게 말하는 연습을 하는 것입니다.

이와 같은 능력을 개발하려면, 원어민과 비슷한 속도로 직독직해로 영어를 이해하고, 영어로 표현하는 훈련(동시통역 연습)을 해야 합니다. 다시 말하여 영어를 직독직해로 빠르게 읽는 연습을 하고, 직독직해로 해석한 내용을 보면서 영어로 말하는 연습(동시통역 연습)을 꾸준히 실천합니다. 이런 목적을 성취하도록 『오헨리 단편선』을 직독직해로 읽고, 연습문제에서 동시통역 연습을 할 수 있도록 교재를 구성했습니다. 아래에 제시된 단계에 따라 공부하면, 영어 실력이 빠르게 향상됩니다.

Step 1 영어 어순대로 이해하기

원서를 직독직해로 읽는 능력을 키우려면, 영어 어순대로 읽는 능력과 풍부한 어휘력이 필요합니다. 먼저 『오헨리 단편선』을 직독직해로 읽으면서 영어 어순대로 읽고 이해하는 연습을 합니다. 이야기를 읽는 동안 모르는 어휘나 이해하기 어려운 문장이 나오면, 중요한 의미만 파악하고, 빠르게 읽고 이해합니다. 본 교재를 두 번째로 읽을 때, 모르는 어휘를 익히고, 어려운 문장을 좀 더 정확히 이해합니다. 때로는 모르는 어휘와 문장을 단번에 모두 익히겠다고 지나치게 욕심을 부리면, 오히려 학습에 흥미가 떨어지고 지속적으로 공부할 수 없게 됩니다. 개인에 따라 차이가 있지만, 본 교재를 세 번 또는 네 번 읽으면서 모르는 어휘와 문장과 친숙해지면, 몰랐던 단어를 쉽게 익힐 수 있습니다. 게다가 어렵게 느껴졌던 문장도 쉽게 이해됩니다.

Step 2 원어민 속도로 읽기

　직독직해로 읽는 연습을 한 다음엔 원어민과 같은 속도로 읽는 연습을 해야 합니다. 이러한 속독 연습을 할 수 있도록 해설 없는 『오헨리 단편선』을 후반부에 수록했습니다. 이 부분을 반복해서 읽으면, 빠르게 읽는 연습을 할 수 있기 때문입니다. 속독을 권장하는 이유는 두 가지가 있습니다. 첫째 영어 어순대로 이해하는 능력을 키워야 원어민과 비슷한 속도로 읽고 이해할 수 있기 때문입니다. 둘째 읽기 속도가 빨라져야 듣기가 즐겁고 편해지기 때문입니다.

Step 3 원어민 수준으로 듣고 이해하기

　영어로 쓰인 이야기를 말하는 속도로 읽고 이해할 수 있으면, 원어민이 말하는 속도로 이해하는 연습에 들어갑니다. 그것은 MP3를 들으면서 원어민처럼 소설을 자연스럽게 이해하는 것입니다. 이런 연습을 반복 하면, 원어민이 빠르게 말하는 문장을 들으면서 이해할 수 있습니다. 이렇게 듣자마자 이해하는 능력을 키워야 유창하게 회화를 할 수 있는 기반이 마련됩니다.

Step 4 동시통역 연습

　연습문제 중 동시통역을 연습할 수 있는 부분이 있습니다. 동시통역이란 입으로 영작하는 연습입니다. 즉 직독직해로 해석된 문장을 보자마자 영어로 유창하게 말하는 것입니다. 유창하게 영어로 말하려면, 읽고 이해하는 것보다 더 많은 노력과 연습이 필요합니다. 혼자서 영어 회화 연습을 할 때 활용하면, 매우 효과적인 영어 공부방법입니다.

　하지만 동시통역 연습을 제대로 활용하려면, 세 가지 어려움을 극복해야 합니다. 첫째 영어 문장을 만들 때 필요한 단어를 뜸들이지 않고 생각해 내는 것입니다. 둘째 쉬운 문법을 제대로 활용하는 것입니다. 세 번째 자연스럽고 유창하게 발음하는 것입니다. 이런 연습을 꾸준히 하면, 읽기 속도가 빨라지고, 빠르게 듣고 이해할 수 있으며, 유창하게 말할 수 있습니다. 동시통역 연습을 실천하면, 원어민 수준으로 읽고 말할 수 있게 됩니다.

퀴즈 가이드

『오헨리 단편선』을 읽으며 동시에 복습할 수 있도록 퀴즈를 만들어 놓았습니다. 모두 11개의 퀴즈로 구성되어 있습니다. 본문을 이해하고 본문에 나온 문장을 통해 영어 실력을 입체적으로 키우기 바랍니다.

* 퀴즈의 구성

각 퀴즈는 모두 4개의 파트(A. 내용 이해하기, B. 단어, C. 직독직해, D. 동시통역)로 구성되어 있습니다. 내용을 이해한 다음에 주요 단어를 복습하고 다시 직독직해 연습을 한 다음에 최종적으로 동시통역 연습을 통해서 입으로 영작하는 연습을 하기 바랍니다.

* 퀴즈의 사용방법
A. 내용 이해하기

본문의 내용을 잘 이해하셨는지 체크하기 위해 간단한 질문을 만들었습니다. 내용이 본문과 일치하면 T(True), 틀리면 F(False)를 표기하시면 됩니다.

B. 단어

영어로 설명된 정의에 어울리는 단어를 찾는 것입니다. 적당한 단어를 보기에서 선택하도록 했습니다. 단어 설명을 영문으로 한 까닭은 영어로 설명된 단어의 정의에 익숙해지면, 회화를 할 때 영어로 유창하게 설명할 수 있기 때문입니다.

C. 직독직해

본문에 나오는 문장 중에서 약간 까다롭거나 구조가 복잡한 문장을 4개씩 골랐습니다. 영어의 어순대로 읽고 이해하는 훈련을 한 번 더 해보기 바랍니다.

D. 동시통역

영어의 어순대로 한글로 제시하고, 한글 해석을 보면서 영어로 작문(동시통역)을 연습하는 파트입니다. 처음에는 힘이 들겠지만 문자로 영작하는 것보다 입으로 바로 말하는 것이 효과적입니다.

목차

The Last Leaf (마지막 잎새)

SCENE **1**	track 02	22
SCENE **2**	track 02	24
SCENE **3**	track 02	26
SCENE **4**	track 02	28
SCENE **5**	track 02	30
SCENE **6**	track 02	32
Quiz 1		34
SCENE **7**	track 02	36
SCENE **8**	track 02	38
SCENE **9**	track 02	40
SCENE **10**	track 02	42
SCENE **11**	track 02	44
SCENE **12**	track 02	46
Quiz 2		48

After Twenty Years (20년 후)

SCENE **1**	track 03	50
SCENE **2**	track 03	52

CONTENTS

SCENE **3**	track 03	54
SCENE **4**	track 03	56
SCENE **5**	track 03	58
SCENE **6**	track 03	60
Quiz 3		62

The Gift of the Magi (현자의 선물)

SCENE **1**	track 04	64
SCENE **2**	track 04	66
SCENE **3**	track 04	68
SCENE **4**	track 04	70
SCENE **5**	track 04	72
Quiz 4		74

SCENE **6**	track 04	76
SCENE **7**	track 04	78
SCENE **8**	track 04	80
SCENE **9**	track 04	82
SCENE **10**	track 04	84
Quiz 5		86

Two Thanksgiving Day Gentlemen (추수감사절의 두 신사)

SCENE **1**	track 05	88
SCENE **2**	track 05	91
SCENE **3**	track 05	94
SCENE **4**	track 05	96
Quiz 6		98
SCENE **5**	track 05	100
SCENE **6**	track 05	102
SCENE **7**	track 05	104
SCENE **8**	track 05	106
Quiz 7		108

A Retrieved Reformation (개과천선)

SCENE **1**	track 06	110
SCENE **2**	track 06	113
SCENE **3**	track 06	115
SCENE **4**	track 06	117
SCENE **5**	track 06	120
SCENE **6**	track 06	122
Quiz 8		124

SCENE **7**	track 06	126
SCENE **8**	track 06	129
SCENE **9**	track 06	132
SCENE **10**	track 06	134
SCENE **11**	track 06	136
Quiz 9		138

The Cop and the Anthem (경찰과 찬송가)

SCENE **1**	track 07	140
SCENE **2**	track 07	144
SCENE **3**	track 07	146
SCENE **4**	track 07	148
Quiz 10		150
SCENE **5**	track 07	152
SCENE **6**	track 07	154
SCENE **7**	track 07	156
SCENE **8**	track 07	159
SCENE **9**	track 07	162
Quiz 11		164

O. Henry's Short Stories를 다시 읽어 보세요. 166

THE LAST LEAF
마지막 잎새

SCENE 1

In a little district / west of Washington Square /
작은 지역에서는 /   워싱턴 광장의 서쪽의

the streets have run crazy /
도로들은 복잡하게 되어 있다 /

and broken themselves into small strips / called "places."
그리고 작은 길로 쪼개져 있다 /   '플레이스' 라고 불리는

These "places" make strange angles and curves.
이러한 '플레이스'는 이상한 각도와 곡선을 만든다

One street crosses itself a time or two.
하나의 길이 한두 번은 다시 그 길로 교차한다

An artist once discovered / a valuable possibility in this street.
어느 예술가가 예전에 발견한 적이 있었다 /   이 거리에서 귀중한 가능성을

Suppose / a collector with a bill for paints, paper and canvas should, / in walking down this street, /
상상해보아라 (어떤 상황을?) / 물감, 종이, 캔버스 값을 받으러 온 사람이 /   이 길을 통과하는 동안 /

suddenly meet / himself coming back, /
갑자기 경험하게 되는 것(상황)을 / 자기 자신이 되돌아오고 있다는 것을 /

without receiving a cent!
1센트도 받지 못한 채로!

So, to quaint old Greenwich Village /
그래서 별나고 구닥다리인 그리니치 마을로 /

the art people soon came prowling, / hunting for /
예술가들이 곧 어슬렁거리며 들어왔다 /   (그리고) 찾아다녔다 /

north windows / and eighteenth-century gables and
북향의 창문을 /   그리고 18세기 풍의 박공지붕과

Dutch attics and low rents.
네덜란드식 다락방과 싼 셋집을

Then they imported / some pewter mugs /
그리고는 그들은 가지고 들어왔다 / 백랍 머그잔을 /

and a chafing dish or two / from Sixth avenue,
그리고 요리용 냄비 한두 개를 / 6번가에서

and became a "colony."
그래서 화가 마을이 되었다

At the top of a squatty, three-story building /
땅딸막한 3층 건물 제일 위층에 /

Sue and Johnsy had their studio.
수와 존시가 화실을 갖고 있었다

"Johnsy" was familiar for Joanna.
'존시'는 조앤나의 애칭이었다

One of the two young women was from Maine;
두 젊은 여성 가운데 한명은 메인 주 출신이고,

the other from California.
다른 여성은 캘리포니아 출신이다

They had met / at a restaurant of Eighth street /
그들은 만났었다 / 8번가의 한 식당에서 /

called "Delmonico's," / and found /
'델모니코' 라고 불리는 / 그리고 발견했다 /

their tastes in art, food, and clothes / so congenial /
예술, 음식, 옷에 대한 취향이 / 너무나 비슷하다는 것을 /

that the joint studio resulted.
그래서 그들의 공동 화실이 생겼다

---

district 지역 run crazy 미친 듯이 달리다(복잡하게 되어있다) strip (상점이 늘어서 있는) 가로, 길
discover 발견하다 valuable 귀중한, 가치 있는 possibility 가능성 suppose 상상하다 collector 수금원
meet 경험하다 quaint 별난, 기묘한 prowl 어슬렁거리다 gable 박공지붕 attic 다락방 import 가지고 들어오다
pewter 백랍(양은) chafing dish 요리용 냄비 colony ~인 거리, 거주 지역 squatty 땅딸막한
familiar 격식을 차리지 않은, 친밀한 congenial 취미가 같은

SCENE 2

That was in May.
그런 일은 5월에 발생했다

In November a cold, unseen stranger, /
11월에 차갑고 보이지 않는 낯선 사람이 /

whom the doctors called Pneumonia, /
(그 낯선 사람을) 의사들은 폐렴이라고 불렀던 /

stalked about the colony, / touching one here and there /
(그는) 화가 마을 여기저기를 활보했다 /   (그리고) 여기저기서 사람들을 건드리며 /

with his icy fingers. Over on the east side /
차가운 손가락으로   화가 마을 동쪽에서 /

this ravager strode boldly, / attacking his victims by scores, /
이 파괴자는 큰 걸음으로 대담하게 걸었다 / (그러면서) 수십 명의 희생자를 공격했다 /

but his feet trod slowly / through the maze /
그러나 천천히 걸었다 /   미로를 통과할 때 /

of the narrow and moss-grown "places."
좁고   이끼가 자란 '플레이스'라는

Mr. Pneumonia was not /
폐렴이라는 사람은 아니었다 /

what you would call a chivalric old gentleman.
여러분들이 예의가 바르고 나이 많은 신사라고 부르고 싶은 분이

A little woman from California /
캘리포니아 출신의 작고 어린 여인은 /

was hardly fair game / for the red-fisted, /
좋은 사냥감이 되지 않았다 /   피가 묻은 주먹을 휘두르며 /

short-breathed old gentleman?
숨을 헐떡거리는 늙은 신사에겐

But Johnsy he smote; and she lay, / scarcely moving, /
그러나 존시를 그는 공격했다 그래서 그녀는 드러누웠고 / 거의 움직이지 못한 채로 /

on her painted iron bedstead, / looking /
페인트로 칠한 철제 침대에서 /   (그리고) 바라보고 있었다 /

through the small Dutch window-panes /
작은 네덜란드 풍의 유리창을 통하여 /

at the blank wall of the next brick house.
(무엇을 바라보았나?) 이웃 벽돌집의 빈 벽을

24 O. Henry's Short Stories

One morning / the busy doctor invited /
어느 날 아침 /   바쁜 의사는 불렀다 /

Sue into the hallway / with a shaggy, gray eyebrow.
수를 복도로 /   덥수룩한 회색 눈썹을 하고

"She has very small chance," / he said, /
그녀는 나을 가능성이 거의 없어 /   그는 말했다 /

as he shook down /
그가 흔들면서 /

the mercury in his clinical thermometer.
체온계의 수은주를

Pneumonia 폐렴 stalk 활보하다 ravager 파괴자 strode (stride-strode-stridden) 대담하게 걷다
victim 희생자, 피해자 by scores 수십 명씩 tread 걷다, 가다 maze 미로 moss-grown 이끼가 자란
chivalric 기사도의 hardly 거의 ~하지 않다 game 사냥감 red-fisted 피가 묻은 주먹을 휘두르는
smite (smite-smote-smitten) 강타하다, 공격하다 scarcely 거의 ~아니다 bedstead 침대의 뼈대
invite 부르다, 초대하다 shaggy 텁수룩한 mercury 수은 clinical thermometer 체온계

SCENE 3

"And that chance is / for her to want to live.
그리고 (그녀가 회복할) 가능성이란 / 그녀가 살려는 의지예요

Sometimes when people have waited for the undertaker, /
때때로 사람들이 장의사나 기다리고 있으면 /

it doesn't matter / what prescriptions I give.
중요하지 않아요 /   어떤 처방을 내가 하는지는

Your little lady has made up her mind /
당신의 어린 소녀는 판단을 내렸다 /

that she's not going to get well.
(어떤 판단을?) 그녀는 낫지 않을 것이라고

Has she anything on her mind?"
그녀는 무슨 생각을 하고 있는 거지?

"She -she wanted to paint / the Bay of Naples some day,"
그녀 - 그녀는 그리고 싶어 했어요 /   언젠가 나폴리의 만을

said Sue. "Paint? -bosh! Has she anything on her mind /
수는 말했다.   그림을 그린다고? 무슨 헛소리! 그녀는 뭔가 생각하고 있나 /

worth thinking about twice / - a man for instance?"
두 번이라도 생각할 만한 가치가 있는 /   예를 들어 남자문제 같은 것을?

"A man?" said Sue, / with a jew's twang in her voice.
남자라고?   수가 말했다 /   유태인 식 코맹맹이 소리로

"Is a man worth -but, no, doctor; there is nothing of the kind."
남자가 그럴 만한 가치가 - 그러나 아니 선생님   그런 것은 없어요

"Well, it is the weakness, then," said the doctor.
음, 그렇다면 그건 약점이군   의사가 말했다

"I will do all / that science can accomplish /
내가 모든 수단을 다 해볼게 / 과학이 이룰 수 있는 /

as much as possible.
가능하다면

But whenever my patient begins to count /
그러나 내 환자가 세기 시작할 때마다 /

the carriages in her funeral procession /
그녀의 장례식 행렬에 마차의 수를 /

I subtract 50 percent / from the curative power of medicines.
나는 50퍼센트를 뺀다 /   약의 치유 효과로부터

If you will get / her to ask one question /
자네가 (~하게) 할 수 있다면 / 그녀가 질문하도록 /

about the new winter styles in cloak sleeves, /
이번 겨울에 나올 외투의 소매 스타일에 대해 /

I will promise you / a one-in-five chance for her, /
저는 당신에게 약속하겠습니다. / 20퍼센트의 가능성이 있다고 /

instead of one in ten."
10퍼센트가 아닌

Key Expression

"get" 동사가 "누군가에게 어떤 일을 시키다"라는 의미로 쓰이면, "have", "make"보다 약하게 강요한다. "get" 동사에는 "누군가에게 설득하거나 권유하여 어떤 일을 시키다"라는 의미가 있다. 또한 "have", "make" 동사가 "누군가에게 어떤 일을 시키다"라는 의미로 쓰일 때는 사람에게 "강요하여 어떤 일을 시키다"라는 의미가 있다. 즉 "have", "make" 동사에는 상대방에게 압력을 가하여 강제적으로 어떤 일을 시키는 뜻이 있다. 하지만 "get" 동사가 "시키다"라는 의미로 쓰이면, 상대방을 권유하거나 설득하여 어떤 일을 하게 하는 의미가 있다.

ex) Will you get her to help me?
　　설득할 수 있어요 / 그녀가 나를 돕도록
　　I can't get her to sing the agreement.
　　나는 설득할 수 없다 / 그녀가 합의서에 서명하도록
　　I'll get my daughter to prepare lunch.
　　내가 설득할게 / 딸이 점심을 준비하도록

---

undertaker 장의사 prescription 처방 make up one's mind 판단을 내리다, 결심하다 bosh 헛소리
twang 콧소리, 코맹맹이 소리 accomplish 이루다 funeral procession 장례식 행렬 subtract 빼다
curative 치유적인 cloak sleeves 외투의 소매

SCENE 4

After the doctor had gone / Sue went into the workroom
의사가 가버린 후 /   수는 작업실로 들어가서 울었다 /

and cried / a Japanese napkin to a pulp.
       일본산 냅킨이 완전히 젖도록

Then she swaggered into Johnsy's room /
그 다음 그녀는 거들먹거리며 존시의 방으로 들어갔다 /

with her drawing board, / whistling ragtime.
화판을 들고 /   (그리고) 휘파람으로 재즈를 부르면서

Johnsy lay, / scarcely making a ripple /
존시는 누웠다 / (어떻게 누워있었나?) 시트에 거의 주름이 생기지 않게 /

under the bedclothes, / with her face toward the window.
시트 아래에서 /   (게다가) 얼굴을 창문 쪽으로 향한 채

Sue stopped whistling, / thinking / she was asleep.
수는 휘파람을 그만 불었다 / 생각했기 때문에 / 그녀가 자고 있다고

She arranged her board / and began a pen-and-ink drawing /
그녀는 화판을 준비했다 /   그리고 펜과 잉크로 그리기 시작했다 /

to illustrate a magazine story.
잡지 스토리용 삽화로 넣으려고

Young artists must pave their way / to Art /
젊은 화가들은 스스로 길을 개척해야 한다 /   예술로 향하는

by drawing pictures for magazine stories /
(어떻게?) 잡지 스토리용 삽화를 그림을 그려서 /

that young authors write / to pave their way to Literature.
(그 잡지 스토리를) 젊은 작가가 쓴다 / 문학으로 향하는 길을 개척하기 위해

As Sue was sketching / a pair of elegant horseshow riding
수가 스케치하고 있었을 때 /   한 벌의 근사한 말품평회용 바지와

trousers and a monocle / on the figure of the hero, /
              외알 안경을 /   스토리 주인공의 모습에 /

an Idaho cowboy, / she heard a low sound, /
(주인공은) 아이다호 카우보이인 / 그녀는 낮은 소리를 들었다 /

several times repeated. She went quickly / to the bedside.
몇 번 반복되는   그녀는 재빨리 갔다 /   침대 곁으로

Johnsy's eyes were open wide.
존시의 눈은 크게 떠있었다

She was looking out the window and counting, /
그녀는 창문 밖을 바라보면서 세고 있었다 /

counting backward. "Twelve," she said, / and a little later
거꾸로 세면서   12   그녀가 말했다 / 그리고 조금 뒤에

"eleven;" / and then "ten," / and "nine;" / and then "eight"
11 /   그런 다음에는 10 / 그리고 9 /   그 다음은   8

and "seven," / almost together.
그리고 7 /   거의 동시에

Sue looked anxiously / out of the window.
수는 걱정스럽게 바라보았다 /   창문 밖을

What was there / to count?
무엇이었을까 /   셀만 한 것이

There was only a bare, dreary yard / to be seen, /
비어있는 쓸쓸한 마당만이 있었다 /   눈에 보이는 /

and the blank wall of the brick house / twenty feet, away.
그리고 벽돌집의 빈 벽이 있었다 /   20피트 떨어진 곳에

An old, old ivy vine, / gnarled and decayed at the roots, /
아주 오래된 담쟁이덩굴이 /   옹이가 생기고 뿌리부분이 썩은 /

climbed / half way up the brick wall.
타고 올라가 있었다 / 벽돌 벽의 절반까지

Key Expression

관계대명사(that)와 선행사의 관계를 이해한다.

Young artists must pave their way / to Art /
젊은 화가들은 길을 개척해야 한다 / (어떤 길?) 예술로 향하는
"pave the way"를 글자그대로 해석하면, "도로를 포장하다"라는 의미다.
여기서는 비유적으로 사용되어 차량이 이동하는 길이 아니라 "예술"로 향하여 가는 길을 의미한다.

by drawing pictures / for magazine stories /
(어떻게?) 그림을 그려서 / (어떤 그림?) 잡지 스토리용 삽화를 /
"by 동사ing"형태는 "어떤 일을 하는 방법"을 설명할 때 사용한다.

that young authors write / to pave their way to Literature.
(그 잡지 스토리를) 젊은 작가가 쓴다 / (왜) 문학으로 향하는 길을 개척하기 위해
"that"이라는 관계대명사는 바로 앞에 나온 "magazine stories"를 가리킨다.
그리고 "that"은 "write" 동사의 목적어 역할을 한다.

---

pulp 걸쭉한 상태, 흐물흐물한 상태 swagger 거들먹거리며 걷다 ripple 천 따위의 주름, 잔물결
bedclothes 침구, 시트 illustrate 삽화나 그림을 싣다 pave the way to ~로 가는 길을 개척하다
elegant 근사한, 우아한 monocle 외알 안경 anxiously 근심하여 dreary 쓸쓸한 vine 덩굴식물
gnarled 옹이가 있는, 울퉁불퉁한 decay 썩다

29

SCENE 5

The cold breath of autumn had stricken /
가을의 차가운 바람이 쳤었다 /

its leaves from the vine /
담쟁이 잎사귀를 /

until its skeleton branches clung, / almost bare, /
앙상하게 남은 가지가 달라붙어 있을 때까지 / 거의 벌거벗겨져서 /

to the bricks.
벽돌에

"What is it, dear?" asked Sue.
그게 뭐니, 애야   수가 물었다

"Six," said Johnsy, / in almost a whisper.
6   존시가 말했다 /   거의 속삭이듯이

"They're falling faster now.
지금은 점점 더 빨리 떨어지고 있어

Three days ago there were almost a hundred.
3일 전에는 거의 백 개가 있었어.

It hurt my head / to count them.
머리를 아프게 해 (무엇이) / 잎사귀를 세는 것은

But now it's easy. There goes another one.
그러나 이제는 쉬워   저기 또 하나 떨어진다.

There are only five left now."
이젠 겨우 5개만 남았네

"Five what, dear? Tell your Sue."
다섯 뭐라고, 애야   말해봐

"Leaves. On the ivy vine.
잎을   담쟁이덩굴에 있는

When the last one falls / I must go, too.
마지막 잎사귀가 떨어질 때 /   나도 죽어야 해

I've known that / for three days.
나는 그것을 알고 있었어 / 3일 전부터

Didn't the doctor tell you?"
의사가 너에게 이야기해주지 않았어

"Oh, I never heard of such nonsense," /
난 그런 말도 안 되는 소리를 들어본 적이 없어 /

complained Sue, / with scorn.
수가 불평했다 / 조롱하는 말투로

"What have old ivy leaves to do with / your getting well?
담쟁이덩굴 잎사귀와 무슨 관련이 있니 / 네가 병이 낫는 것과

And you used to love that vine, / you naughty girl.
그리고 너는 담쟁이를 좋아했었잖아 / 넌 장난꾸러기 소녀야

Don't be a little fool.
바보 같은 소리하지 마

Key Expression

동사의 쓰임새란?

The cold breath of autumn had stricken / its leaves / from the vine /
가을의 차가운 바람이 쳤었다 (무엇을 때렸느냐?) / 잎사귀를 / (어떤 잎사귀?) 담쟁이 덩굴의
"stricken" 다음에는 무엇을 때렸는지를 나타내는 "leaves"가 나온다.

until its skeleton branches clung, almost bare, / to the bricks.
(언제까지?) 앙상하게 남은 가지가 달라붙어 있을 때까지 / (어디에 매달려 있나?) 거의 벌거벗겨져서 / (어디에 매달려 있나?) 벽돌에
"until"은 앞에서 나온 동작이 "언제까지" 지속되는지 보여준다.

Used to; 1. 과거에 ~하곤 했다(현재와 다른 과거의 습관을 표현한다.)

ex) I used to drink a lot.
나는 술을 마시곤 했다(현재는 잘 안 마신다)

2. 이전은 ~였다(현재와 다른 과거의 상태를 표현한다.)

ex) There used to be a restaurant on the corner.
이전에 있었다 / 식당이 / 저 모퉁이에(현재는 없다)

breath 미풍, 산들바람 strike (strike-struck-stricken) 치다, 때리다 skeleton 앙상한 사람(물건)
clung (cling-clung-clung) 달라붙다 bare 발가벗은 whisper 속삭임 complain 불평하다
with scorn 조롱하는 말투로 naughty 장난꾸러기인

SCENE 6

Why, the doctor told me this morning /
글쎄, 의사가 오늘 아침에 나한테 말했어. /

that your chances for getting well real soon were /
(뭐라고) 네가 곧 나을 가능성은 /

-let's see exactly what he said- /
정확히 뭐라고 했었지 /

he said / the chances were ten to one!
그는 말했지 / 열에 하나라고 했어!

Why, that's almost as good a chance /
글쎄   그건 (사고당할) 위험률과 거의 같아 /

as we have in New York / when we ride on the street cars /
우리가 뉴욕에 사는 동안 /   전차를 탈 때나 /

or walk past a new building.
혹은 신축 빌딩을 걸어지나갈 때

Try to take some broth now, / and let Sudie go back to her
스프를 좀 먹어라 /   그리고 수디가 그림을 다시 그리게 해라 /

drawing, / so she can sell the editor man with it, /
          그래서 그녀가 그림을 편집자에게 팔 수 있게 /

and buy port wine / for her sick child, /
그리고 포르투갈 와인을 살 수 있게 / 그녀의 아픈 아이에게 /

and pork chops / for her greedy self."
그리고 돼지고기를 살 수 있도록 / 욕심 많은 그녀에게는

"You needn't get any more wine," said Johnsy, /
너는 더 이상 와인이 필요 없어   존시가 말했다 /

keeping her eyes fixed / out the window.
시선을 고정시킨 채로 /   창문 밖으로

"There goes another. No, I don't want any broth.
또 하나 떨어진다   아니야, 나는 스프가 싫어

That leaves just four. I want to see / the last one fall /
이젠 4개만 남았어   나는 보고 싶어 /   마지막 잎사귀가 떨어지는 것을 /

before it gets dark. Then I'll go, too."
어두워지기 전에   그러면 나도 죽을 거야

"Johnsy, dear," said Sue, / bending over her, /
존시   애야   수가 말했다 /   그녀에게 몸을 굽히며 /

"will you promise me / to keep your eyes closed, /
  나에게 약속할래 /   너의 눈을 감은 채로 있겠다고 /

and not look out the window / until I am done working?
그리고 창문 밖을 쳐다보지 않겠다고 /   내가 일을 끝낼 때까지

I must hand those drawings in / by tomorrow.
나는 이 그림들을 제출해야해 /   내일까지

I need the light, / or I would draw the shade down."
나는 전등이 필요해 /   그렇지 않으면 나는 커튼을 칠거야

"Couldn't you draw / in the other room?" asked Johnsy, /
  그리면 안 되니 /   다른 방에서   존시가 물었다 /

coldly. "I'd rather be here / by you," said Sue.
냉정하게   그냥 여기에 있을 거야 /   네 옆에   수가 말했다

"Besides I don't want / you to keep looking /
  게다가 나는 마음에 안 들어 /   네가 계속 바라보는 것이 /

at those silly ivy leaves."
그 바보스러운 담쟁이 잎사귀를

Key Expression

as good as; ~와 같은 비슷한

ex) She as good as promised me the job.
    그녀는 약속한 것과 비슷해 / 나에게 그 일자리를 (주겠다고)

broth 묽은 스프 port wine 포르투갈 와인(포르투갈 제품으로 진홍색의 단맛이 도는 와인이며 port는 Portuguese의 줄임말임) greedy 욕심 많은

Quiz 1

A. 내용 이해하기

다음 문장을 읽고 본문의 내용과 맞으면 T(True), 틀리면 F(False)를 쓰세요.

1. Sue lay on a bed because Pneumonia attacked her.
2. If Johnsy counts the leaves on the ivy vine, her head hurts.
3. The doctor said that the possibility of Johnsy's recovery was affected by her will to live.
4. Johnsy lost her appetite because she was on a diet.

B. 단어

다음 제시된 단어의 설명을 읽고, 어떤 단어의 정의를 설명하는지 아래의 박스에서 찾아 써 보세요.

1. always wanting something more than you need
2. a man whose job arranges funerals
3. a complicated and confusing arrangement of streets
4. an area of a town or city with particular features
5. able to cure illness
6. not willing to obey adults and behaving badly
7. pleasant to spend time with someone because you feel comfortable and relaxed
8. attractive in an unusual way
9. beautiful, attractive, or graceful
10. making you feel sad or bored
11. to walk proudly and confidently
12. to find something you did not expect to find
13. an official piece of paper on which a doctor writes the type of medicine a patient should take

> district quaint discover congenial maze greedy naughty
> prescription curative undertaker swagger elegant dreary

Answer

A. 1. F 2. T 3. T 4. F
B. 1. greedy 2. undertaker 3. maze 4. district 5. curative 6. naughty 7. congenial 8. quaint 9. elegant 10. dreary 11. swagger 12. discover 13. prescription

C. 직독직해

아래에 제시된 문장을 직독직해로 해석해보세요.

1. One morning / the busy doctor invited / Sue into the hallway / with a shaggy, gray eyebrow.

   →

2. After the doctor had gone / Sue went into the workroom and cried / a Japanese napkin to a pulp.

   →

3. There was only a bare, dreary yard / to be seen, / and the blank wall of the brick house / twenty feet, away.

   →

4. The cold breath of autumn had stricken / its leaves from the vine / until its skeleton branches clung, almost bare, / to the bricks.

   →

D. 동시통역

아래에 제시된 직독직해를 보고, 영어로 말해보세요.

1. 어느 예술가가 예전에 발견한 적이 있었다. / 이 거리에서 귀중한 가능성을

   →

2. 그녀는 뭔가 생각하고 있나 / 두 번이라도 생각할 만한 가치가 있는?

   →

3. 내가 모든 수단을 다 해볼게 / 과학이 이룰 수 있는 / 가능하다면

   →

4. 그녀는 창문 밖을 바라보면서 세고 있었다 / 거꾸로 세면서

   →

Answer

C. 1. 어느 날 아침 / 바쁜 의사는 불렀다 / 수를 복도로 / 덥수룩한 회색 눈썹을 하고 2. 의사가 가버린 후 / 수는 작업실로 들어가서 울었다 / 일본산 냅킨이 완전히 젖도록 3. 비어있는 쓸쓸한 마당만이 있었다 / 눈에 보이는 것은 / 그리고 벽돌집의 빈 벽이 있었다 / 20피트 떨어진 곳에 4. 가을의 차가운 바람이 쳤다 / 담쟁이 잎사귀를 / 앙상하게 남은 가지가 달라붙어 있을 때까지 / 거의 벌거벗겨져서 / 벽돌에

D. 1. An artist once discovered / a valuable possibility in this street. 2. Has she anything on her mind / worth thinking about twice? 3. I will do all / that science can accomplish / as much as possible. 4. She was looking out the window and counting, / counting backward.

SCENE 7

"Tell me / as soon as you have finished," said Johnsy, /
알려줘 / 끝나는 대로 곧 존시가 말했다

closing her eyes, and lying / white and still /
눈을 감고 누워서 / 창백하고 조용히 /

as a fallen statue, / "because I want to see /
쓰러진 조각처럼 왜냐하면 나는 보고 싶어 /

the last one fall.
마지막 잎사귀가 떨어지는 것을.

I'm tired of waiting. I'm tired of thinking.
나는 기다리는 것에 지쳤어. 나는 생각하는 것도 지쳤어.

I want to turn loose / my hold on everything, /
나는 버리기를 원해 / 모든 것에 대한 집착(미련)을 /

and go sailing down, down, /
그리고 점점 아래로 내려가고 싶어 /

just like one of those poor, tired leaves."
바로 저 불쌍하고 지친 잎사귀처럼

"Try to sleep," said Sue.
잠을 좀 청해 봐 수가 말했다

"I must call Behrman up / to be my model /
나는 버먼씨에게 요청할거야 / 모델을 해달라고 /

for the old hermit miner. I'll not be gone a minute.
은둔하는 늙은 광부의 금방 돌아올게

Don't try to move / till I come back."
움직이려고 하지 마 / 내가 돌아올 때까지

Old Behrman was a painter / who lived /
늙은 버먼씨는 화가였다 / (어떤 화가?) 살고 있었던 /

on the ground floor beneath them. He was past sixty /
(어디에) 그들의 아래층인 1층에 그는 60세가 넘었다

and had / a Michael Angelo's Moses beard / curling down.
그리고 있었다 / 미켈란젤로의 모세와 같은 수염이 / 곱슬곱슬하게 감겨 내려진

Behrman was a failure / in art.
버먼씨는 실패자였다 예술에선

Forty years he had wielded the brush /
40년 동안 그는 붓을 휘둘렀다(그림을 그렸다) /

without getting near /
근처에도 가지 못한 채로 /

enough to touch the hem of his Mistress's robe.
(예술의) 여신의 옷자락을 만질 정도로

He had been always about to / paint a masterpiece, /
그는 언제나 준비가 되어 있는 것 같았다 /   걸작을 그릴

but had never yet begun it.
그러나 아직 전혀 시작도 안했다.

For several years / he had painted nothing /
수년간 /   그는 어떤 그림도 그리지 않았다 /

except now and then a daub /
가끔 그린 서투른 그림을 제외하곤 /

in the line of commerce or advertising.
상업용이나 광고용 분야에

He earned a little / by serving as a model /
그는 적은 돈을 벌었다 /   (어떻게?) 모델이 되어 /

to those young artists / in the colony /
젊은 화가들을 위한 /   화가 마을에 사는 /

who could not pay the price of a professional.
(어떤 화가?) 전문적인 모델을 사용하는 비용을 지불할 수 없는

Key Expression

"enough" 의 여러 쓰임새를 쉽게 익히는 방법이란?

"enough"란 단어는 형용사로 명사를 설명할 경우엔, 어떤 목적이나 욕구를 충족시키기에 "충분한"이라는 의미로 명사 앞에 온다. 그리고 "어떤 일을 할 정도로, ~할 만큼 충분한"이라는 의미로 쓰이면, 형용사 뒤에 온다. 마지막으로 "enough"는 "어느 정도", "그런대로"라는 의미로 쓰이는 경우도 있다. 쉽게 이해하려면, 복잡하게 문법을 따지기보다 예문을 통하여 무엇이 충분한지 이해할 수 있으면 된다.

ex) He has enough gas to drive up to Seoul.
그는 충분한 연료가 있다 / (뭐하는데?) 서울까지 운전해서 가는데
This house is large enough for us.
이집은 충분히 크다 / (뭐하는데?) 우리가 사는데
He was old enough to vote.
그는 충분히 나이 들었다 / (뭐하는데?) 투표할 만큼
His son is an honest fellow enough.
그의 아들은 정직한 녀석이야 / 어느 정도

---

statue 조각 hermit 은둔자 miner 광부 curl down 말려 내려가다 wield 휘두르다
hem 옷자락, 옷의 가장자리 daub 서투른 그림 line 분야, 업종 commerce 상업 professional 전문가

SCENE 8

He drank gin to excess, / and still talked of his coming
그는 (양주)진을 지나치게 마셨다 / 그리고 그가 그릴 걸작에 대해 여전히 말했다

masterpiece. Also / he was a fierce little old man, /
게다가 / 그는 작고 사나운 노인이었다 /

who scoffed terribly / at softness in any one, /
(그리고 그는) 심하게 비웃었다 / 누구든 연약한 점을 보이면 /

and who regarded / himself as a special guardian /
(그리고 그는) 생각했다 / 자신이 특별한 수호자라고 /

to protect the two young artists / in the studio above.
(어떤 수호자?) 두 명의 젊은 예술가들을 보호하는 / 위층 화실에 사는

Sue found / Behrman smelling strongly of liquor /
수는 발견했다 / 버먼씨가 술 냄새를 강하게 풍기는 것을 /

in his dimly lighted den below.
어둠 침침한 아래층 작업실에서

In one corner / was a blank canvas / on an easel /
한쪽 구석에는 / 아무 그림도 없는 캔버스가 있었다 / 이젤에 걸려 있는 /

that had been waiting there for twenty-five years /
(그 캔버스는?) 25년 동안 거기에 있었던 /

to receive / the first line of the masterpiece.
(왜 기다릴까?) 대우를 받으려고 / 명작의 첫 번째 대열에 속한다는

She told him of Johnsy's fancy, / and how she feared /
그녀는 존시의 환상을 그에게 이야기했다 / 그리고 존시가 얼마나 두려워하는지 (말했다) /

she, / light and fragile as a leaf herself, /
(두려움이란?) 그녀는 / 잎사귀처럼 가볍고 깨지기 쉬운 /

would float away / when her slight hold upon the world /
(그녀는) 날아가 버릴 것이라는 / (언제?) 세상에 대한 가냘픈 의지가 /

grew weaker.
점점 약해지면

Old Behrman, / with his red eyes streaming, /
늙은 버만씨는 / 붉은 눈에 눈물이 글썽거리면서 /

shouted his contempt and derision /
경멸과 조롱을 퍼부었다 /

for such idiotic imaginings.
그런 바보 같은 상상에 대해

"What!" he cried.
무슨 소리! 그는 외쳤다

"Are there such fools? Do people die /
그렇게 어리석은 인간이 있나? / 사람들이 죽을 수 있을까 /

because leaves drop off from a damn vine?
잎사귀가 망할 놈의 담쟁이에서 떨어진다고

I have not heard of such a thing.
나는 그런 소리는 들어본 적이 없다

No, I will not pose as a model / for your dunderhead.
아니, 나는 모델이 되지 않을 거야 / 너희들과 같이 멍청한 바보를 위해

Why do you allow / that silly Johnsy /
왜 너는 내버려 두는 거지 / 그런 바보 같은 존시가 /

to think in such a thing?
어처구니없는 생각을 하도록

That poor little Miss Johnsy."
불쌍한 존시

Key Expression

관계대명사(that)은 무엇을 가리키는가?

In one corner / was / a blank canvas / on an easel /
한쪽 구석에는 / 있었다 / (무엇이?)아무 그림도 없는 캔버스가 / (캔버스는 어디에?) 이젤 위에 /

"was"라는 "be 동사"가 "~이 있다, 존재하다"라는 의미로 사용되면, "was" 다음에는 "a blank canvas"(아무 그림도 없는 캔버스)가 주어로 쓰인다. 그리고 "a blank canvas" 다음에 오는 "on an easel"를 보면, 캔버스가 어디에 있는지 알 수 있다.

that had been waiting there for twenty-five years /
(그 그림 없는 캔버스는 어떤 것일까?) 25년 동안 거기에 있었던 /

"that"은 관계대명사로 앞에 나온 "a blank canvas"를 가리키며, 주어로 사용되었다.

to receive / the first line of the masterpiece.
(왜 기다리고 있었을까?) 대우를 받으려고 / (어떤 대우?) 명작의 첫 번째 대열에 속한다는

"to receive"는 앞에 나온 "waiting"과 연결되어 "왜 기다리고 있는지" 설명해준다.

---

excess 과잉, 초과 fierce 사나운 scoff 비웃다 regard ~이라고 생각하다 liquor 술 den 작업실
receive 대우를 받다 fragile 깨지기 쉬운 stream (눈물이) 흐르다 contempt 경멸 derision 조롱
pose 자세를 취하다 dunderhead 멍청이, 바보 allow ~하도록 내버려 두다

SCENE 9

"She is very ill and weak," said Sue, /
그녀는 매우 아프고 쇠약해요   수가 말했다 /

"and the fever has left /
그리고 열이 (~한 상태가) 되게 했다 /

her mind morbid and full of strange fancies.
그녀의 마음이 병들고 이상한 환상으로 가득 찬 (상태로)

Very well, Mr. Behrman, / if you do not care to pose /
아주 좋아   버먼씨 /   만일 당신이 포즈를 취하고 싶지 않다면 /

for me, / you needn't.
나를 위해 /   그럴 필요 없어요

But I think / you are a horrid old -talkative person."
그러나 나는 생각해 / 당신이 아주 무시무시하고 늙은 수다스러운 사람이라고

"You are just like a woman!" yelled Behrman.
여자란 이래서 탈이야!   버먼이 소리쳤다

"Who said / I will not pose as a model?
누가 말했지 /   내가 모델을 안 해줄 것이라고

Go. I will come with you. For half an hour /
가자. 나도 같이 갈게   30분 전부터 /

I have been trying to say / that I am ready to pose.
나는 말하려고 했었지 /   내가 모델을 할 준비가 되어 있다고.

God! This is not any place /
맙소사! 여기는 장소가 아닌데 /

in which someone so good as Miss Johnsy / lies sick.
(어떤 장소?) 존시양같은 좋은 사람이 /   아파서 누워있을

Some day I will paint a masterpiece, /
언젠가 나는 걸작을 그릴 것이다 /

and we shall all go away. God! yes."
그러면 우리는 모두 여기를 떠날 것이다   좋아!   그렇게 하자

Johnsy was sleeping / when they went upstairs.
존시는 자고 있었다 /   그들이 이층을 갔을 때

Sue pulled / the shade down to the window-sill, /
수는 당겼다 /   커튼을 창문틀까지 /

and motioned / Behrman into the other room.
그리고 몸짓을 했다 /   버먼씨를 다른 방으로 가자고

In there they peered out the window /
거기서 그들은 창밖을 바라보았다 /

fearfully at the ivy vine.
두려운 듯이 담쟁이덩굴을

Then they looked at each other /
그런 다음 그들은 서로 바라보았다 /

for a moment without speaking.
잠시 동안 말없이

A persistent, cold rain was falling, /
끊임없는 차가운 비가 떨어지고 있었다 /

mingled with snow.
눈과 섞여서

Behrman, / in his old blue shirt, /
버먼씨는 / 낡은 청색 셔츠를 입고 있는 /

took his seat as the hermit-miner / on an upturned kettle /
은둔하는 광부처럼 앉았다 / 뒤집은 냄비 위에 /

for a rock. When Sue awoke / from an hour's sleep /
바위 대신에 수가 깨었을 때 / 1시간 자고 /

the next morning she found / Johnsy with wide-open eyes /
다음날 아침 그녀는 발견했다 / 눈을 크게 뜨고 있는 존시가 /

staring at / the drawn green shade.
바라보고 있는 것을 / 내려진 녹색 커튼을

"Pull it up; I want to see," she ordered, / in a whisper.
커튼을 걷어줘 나는 보고 싶어 그녀가 명령했다 / 속삭이는 목소리로

Wearily Sue obeyed.
지쳐서 수는 그녀의 말을 따랐다

> ### Key Expression
>
> **leave; (사람, 사물을) ~한 상태로 두다, ~로 되게 하다**
>
> Leave the door open.
> 두어라 / 문이 열려진 상태로
> The novel was left unfinished.
> 그 소설은 되어있었다 / 끝나지 않은 상태로
> The fever has left / her mind morbid and full of strange fancies.
> 열이 (~한 상태로) 되게 했다 / 그녀의 마음이 병들고 이상한 환상으로 가득 찬 (상태로)

---

morbid 병적인, 불건전한 horrid 무시무시한 talkative 수다스러운 window-sill 창문틀
peer 응시하다, 뚫어지게 바라보다 fearfully 두려운 듯이 persistent 끊임없는 mingle 섞다
upturned 뒤집힌 stare 응시하다

SCENE 10

But, lo! after the beating rain and fierce gusts of wind /
그런데 봐라 후려치는 비와 사나운 바람이 휘몰아친 후에도 /

that had endured through the whole night, /
(그 비바람은) 밤새도록 계속되었지만 /

there yet stood out / against the brick wall / one ivy leaf.
여전히 눈에 띄었다 /   벽돌 벽에는 /   담쟁이 잎사귀 하나가

It was the last on the vine.
그것은 담쟁이의 마지막 잎사귀였다

It was still dark green / near its stem.
그것은 아직도 짙은 녹색이었다 /   잎자루 근처는

But at the edges / it was tinted yellow / with age and decay.
그러나 가장자리는 /   그것은 노랗게 시들었고 /   세월이 흘러 썩으면서

It hung bravely from / a branch /
그것은 용감하게 매달려 있었다 /   가지에 /

some twenty feet above the ground.
땅에서 20피트 위에 있는

"It is the last one," said Johnsy.
이것이 마지막 잎새야   존시가 말했다

"I thought / it would surely fall during the night.
알았는데 /   밤새 틀림없이 떨어질 줄

I heard the wind.
나는 바람 부는 소리를 들었어

It will fall today, / and I shall die / at the same time."
그것은 오늘 떨어질 거야 /   그리고 난 죽을 거야 /   같은 시간에

"Dear, dear!" said Sue, / leaning / her worn face down to the
애야   애야!   수가 말했다 /   기울게 하면서 / 피로한 얼굴을 베개에 /

pillow, / "think of me, if you won't think of yourself.
나를 생각해줘   너 자신을 생각하지 않으려면

What would I do?" But Johnsy did not answer.
나는 어떻게 해야 되니?   그러나 존시는 대답하지 않았다

The most lonely thing in all the world / is a soul /
이 세상에서 가장 쓸쓸한 것은 /   사람이다 /

when it is making ready /
(언제?) 그 사람이 준비를 하고 있을 때 /

to go on its mysterious, far journey.
신비롭고 먼 여행을 떠나려고

The fancy seemed to possess / her more strongly /
이런 상상이 사로잡는 것 같았다 /   그녀를 더욱 강력하게 /

as one by one the ties / that bound /
(~하면서) 하나씩 매듭이 /   (어떤 매듭?) 묶어두었던 /

her to friendship and to earth / were loosed.
그녀를 우정과 이 세상에 /   풀어지면서

The day wore away, / and even through the twilight /
그 날이 저물어 갔고 /   그리고 땅거미가 질 때까지도 /

they could see / the lone ivy leaf clinging /
그들은 볼 수 있었다 /   외로운 담쟁이 잎사귀가 붙어있는 것을 /

to its stem against the wall.
벽에 있는 줄기에

And then, / with the coming of the night /
그리고 나서 /   밤이 다가오자 /

the north wind began to blow, /
북풍이 다시 불어오기 시작했다 /

while the rain still beat against the windows /
비가 여전히 창문을 때렸고 /

and pattered down / from the low Dutch eaves.
후드득 떨어졌던 동안에 /   그리고 낮은 네덜란드 식의 처마에

lo 보라 gust 질풍, 돌풍 stand out 눈에 띄다 stem (식물의) 줄기 soul 사람, 인간 possess 마음을 사로잡다
wear away 시간이 흐르다 patter 후드득 떨어지다 eave 처마

SCENE 11

When it was light enough / Johnsy again commanded /
날이 꽤 밝아지자 /   존시는 또다시 명령했다 /

that the shade be raised. The ivy leaf was still there.
커튼을 걷으라고   담쟁이 잎은 여전히 거기 있었다

Johnsy lay for a long time / looking at it.
존시는 오랫동안 누워있었다 /   그것을 지켜보면서

And then she called to Sue, /
그리고 나서 그녀는 수를 불렀다 /

who was stirring her chicken broth / over the gas stove.
(그때 수는) 닭 스프를 젓고 있었다 /   가스스토브에

"I've been a bad girl, Sudie," said Johnsy.
내가 나쁜 여자였어   수   존시가 말했다

"Something has made / that last leaf stay there /
뭔가가 만든 것이야 /   저 마지막 잎사귀가 계속 저기에 있게 /

to show me / how wicked I was.
(왜?) 나에게 보여주려고 / 내가 얼마나 나쁜가를

It is a sin / to want to die.
죄악이야 /   죽기를 바라는 것은

You may bring me / a little broth now, /
나에게 갖다 줘 /   이제 내게 스프를 좀 /

and some milk / with a little port in it, /
그리고 (갖다 줘) 우유를 /   포르투갈 포도주를 조금 넣어서 /

and -no; bring me a hand-mirror first, /
그리고 아니야; 내게 손거울을 먼저 갖다 줘 /

and then pack / some pillows about me, /
그리고 받쳐줘 /   베개 몇 개를 /

and I will sit up and watch / you cook."
그러면 나는 앉아서 볼 거야 /   네가 요리하는 것을

An hour later she said.
한 시간 뒤에 그녀가 말했다

"Sudie, some day I hope to paint / the Bay of Naples."
수   언젠가 나는 그리고 싶다 /   나폴리의 만을

The doctor came in the afternoon, /
의사가 오후에 들어왔다 /

and Sue had an excuse / to go into the hallway / as he left.
그리고 수는 핑계를 댔다 / (왜?) 복도로 나가려고 / 의사가 나갈 때

"Even chances," said the doctor, /
회복할 가능성이 반이예요, 의사가 말했다 /

taking Sue's thin, shaking hand in his.
수의 마르고 떨리는 손을 잡으면서

"With good nursing / you'll win.
간호를 잘하면 / 당신친구가 병마와 싸워 이길 수 있소

And now I must see / another case / I have downstairs.
그리고 지금 보러가야 해요 / 다른 환자를 / 아래층에 있는

Behrman, his name is - /
버먼   그의 이름이지 /

some kind of an artist, / I believe.
화가라고 /   알고 있어요

Pneumonia, too.
그 사람도 폐렴이죠

He is an old, weak man, /
그는 늙고 허약한 남자이고 /

and the attack of Pneumonia is acute.
폐렴의 발병은 급성이에요

There is no hope for him; /
그에겐 가망이 없지 /

but he goes to the hospital today /
그러나 그는 오늘 병원으로 가요 /

to be made more comfortable."
보다 편안하게 하려고

Key Expression

"make" 동사의 여러 쓰임새를 쉽게 익히는 방법?

"make"동사에는 "사람이 물건을 만들다"는 뜻뿐만 아니라 "사람이나 사건이 어떤 상황을 만들다", "누군가에게 어떤 일을 강제로 시키다"라는 뜻이 있다. 즉 "~에게 ~을 시키다"라는 뜻이나 "~하게 하다"라는 뜻이 된다. 간단하게 사람이 물건을 만드는 것처럼, 어떤 상황을 "만들다"라는 뜻으로 받아들이면, "make"의 의미를 쉽게 이해할 수 있다.

He made me sign the contract.
그는 만들었다 / (어떤 상황을?) 내가 서명하는 / 계약서에

"Something has made / that last leaf stay there.
"원가가 만든 것이야 / (어떤 상황을?) 저 마지막 잎사귀가 계속 저기에 있는

---

enough 상당히, 매우, 꽤 broth 스프 bay 만 case 환자 Pneumonia 폐렴 attack 발병, 발작 acute 급성의

SCENE 12

The next day the doctor said to Sue: /
다음날 의사는 수에게 말했다 /

"She's out of danger. You've won.
그녀는 위험을 벗어났어요   당신이 승리했어요

Nutrition and care now -that's all."
지금은 영양섭취와 간호 -그것만 잘하면 됩니다

And that afternoon / Sue came to the bed /
그리고 그날 오후에 /   수는 침대로 갔다 /

where Johnsy lay, contentedly knitting /
존시가 누워있는   (수는) 만족스럽게 짜고 있었다 /

a very blue and very useless woolen shoulder scarf, /
아주 파랗고 아주 쓸모없는 털 어깨 스카프를 /

and put one arm around her, / pillows and all.
그리고 (수는) 한쪽 팔로 그녀를 껴안았다 /   베개와 모든 것을 (끌어안았다)

"I have something to tell you, white mouse," she said.
너에게 말해줄 것이 있어   하얀 생쥐 같은 아가씨   그녀가 말했다

"Mr. Behrman died of pneumonia / today in the hospital.
버먼씨가 폐렴으로 죽었어 /   오늘 병원에서

He was ill / only two days.
그는 아팠어 /   겨우 2일 동안

The janitor found / him on the morning of the first day /
관리인이 발견했어 / (무엇을?) 그가 첫날 아침에 /

in his room downstairs / helpless with pain.
아래층 그의 방에서 /   고통스러워서 손 쓸 수 없는 (그를)

His shoes and clothing were wet through and icy cold.
그의 신발과 옷은 완전히 젖어서 얼음처럼 차가웠어.

They couldn't imagine / where he had been /
그들은 상상할 수 없었다 / 어디에 있었는지 /

on such a dreadful night.
그가 그렇게 무시무시한 밤에

And then they found / a lantern, / still lighted, /
그리고 나서 그들은 발견했다 /   램프를 /   여전히 불이 켜져 있는 /

and a ladder / that had been dragged from its place, /
그리고 사다리를 (발견했다) / (어떤 사다리?) 원래 있던 곳에서 꺼내온 /

and some scattered brushes, /
그리고 흩어져 있는 붓 몇 개를 (발견했다) /

and a palette / with green and yellow colors mixed on it, /
그리고 팔레트를 (발견했다) / 녹색과 노란색이 섞여 있던 /

and looked / out the window / at the last ivy leaf on the wall.
그리고 봤다 / 창문밖에 있는 / 벽에 있는 마지막 담쟁이 잎사귀를

Didn't you wonder / why it never fluttered or moved /
너는 이상하지 않지 / 왜 저것이 펄럭이거나 움직이지 않는지 /

when the wind blew?
바람이 불 때

Ah, darling, it's Behrman's masterpiece /
아 존시 저건은 버먼씨의 걸작이야 /

- he painted it / there the night / that the last leaf fell."
그는 그림을 그린 것이야 / 저 자리에 밤에 / (어떤 밤?) 마지막 잎사귀가 떨어졌던

Key Expression

"find" 동사는 "뭔가를 발견하다" 라는 의미?

"find" 동사에는 사람이 찾고 있던 물건을 "발견하다"라는 뜻과, 사람이 조사하고 연구하여 어떤 사실을 "발견하다"라는 의미가 있다. 또한 어떤 경험을 하여 그 경험의 의미를 발견하면, "뭔가를 알다"라는 뜻이 있다. 그리고 어떤 사람이 특정한 상황에 처해 있는 것을 알게 되면, "누군가 어떤 상황에 처해 있는 것을 발견하다"라는 의미가 있다. 간단하게 말하면, 뭔가를 발견하게 되는 것이다.

I found the door unlocked.
나는 발견했다(무엇을 발견했나?) / 문이 잠겨있지 않은 (상황을)

The janitor found / him helpless with pain.
관리인이 발견했다 (무엇을 발견했나?) / 그가 아주 고통스러워서 손 쓸 수 없는 (상황을)

nutrition 영양 섭취 contentedly 만족스럽게 janitor (건물의) 관리인 helpless 어찌할 수 없는
dreadful 무시무시한 drag (무거운 것을) 끌다 scatter 흩어지게 하다 flutter 펄럭이다

Quiz 2

A. 내용 이해하기
다음 문장을 읽고 본문의 내용과 맞으면 T(True), 틀리면 F(False)를 쓰세요.

1. Behrman earned money by selling paintings for commercial use.
2. Behrman kept on painting until he made a masterpiece.
3. Johnsy believed she would die if the last leaf on the vine fell.
4. Finally, Behrman finished a masterpiece.

B. 단어
다음 제시된 단어의 설명을 읽고, 어떤 단어의 정의를 설명하는지 아래의 박스에서 찾아 써 보세요.

1. becoming serious or severe quickly
2. someone who, for a religious reason, lives alone and has a simple way of life
3. to make something move gently in the air
4. to laugh at someone or idea; mock
5. to combine with each other
6. to look at something for a long time without moving eyes
7. easily broken or damaged
8. talking a lot
9. to hold tool that you are going to use
10. a sudden strong movement of wind
11. the type of work
12. to move or go quickly in different directions
13. with a strong and unhealthy interest in death

---

hermit wield line scoff fragile morbid talkative
stare gust acute scatter flutter mingle

Answer

A. 1. F 2. F 3. T 4. T

B. 1. acute 2. hermit 3. flutter 4. scoff 5. mingle 6. stare 7. fragile 8. talkative 9. wield 10. gust 11. line 12. scatter 13. morbid

C. 직독직해

아래에 제시된 문장을 직독직해로 해석해보세요.

1. I want to turn loose / my hold on everything, / and go sailing down, / just like one of those poor, tired leaves.

   →

2. In one corner / was a blank canvas / on an easel / that had been waiting there for twenty-five years / to receive / the first line of the masterpiece.

   →

3. God! This is not any place / in which someone so good as Miss Johnsy lies sick.

   →

4. The fancy seemed to possess / her more strongly / as one by one the ties / that bound / her to friendship and to earth / were loosed.

   →

D. 동시통역

아래에 제시된 직독직해를 보고, 영어로 말해보세요.

1. 나는 그런 소리는 들어본 적이 없다.

   →

2. 존시는 자고 있었다 / 그들이 이층을 갔을 때

   →

3. 나는 버먼씨에게 요청할거야 / 모델을 해달라고 / 은둔하는 늙은 광부의

   →

4. 그는 (양주) 진을 많이 마셨다 / 그리고 여전히 걸작을 그릴 것이라고 말했다.

   →

Answer

C. 1. 나는 버리기를 원해 / 모든 것에 대한 집착(미련)을 / 그리고 점점 아래로 내려가고 싶어 / 바로 저 불쌍하고 지친 잎사귀처럼. 2. 한쪽 구석에는 / 아무 그림도 없는 캔버스가 있었다 / 이젤에 걸려 있는 / (그 캔버스는?) 25년 동안 거기에 있었던 / (왜 기다릴까?) 대우를 받으려고 / 명작의 첫 번째 대열에 속한다는
3. 맙소사! 여기는 장소가 아닌데 / (어떤 장소?) 존시양같은 좋은 사람이 아파서 누워있을
4. 이런 상상이 사로잡는 것 같았다 / 그녀를 더욱 강력하게 / (어떻게?) 하나씩 매듭이 / (어떤 매듭?) 묶어두었던 / 그녀를 우정과 이 세상에 / 풀어지면서.
D. 1. I have not heard of such a thing. 2. Johnsy was sleeping / when they went upstairs. 3. I must call Behrman up / to be my model / for the old hermit miner. 4. He drank gin to excess, / and still talked of his coming masterpiece.

After Twenty Years
20년 후

SCENE 1

The policeman on the beat / moved up the avenue /
순찰중인 경찰관 한명이 / 거리를 따라 걸었다 /

impressively. The impressiveness was habitual /
인상적인 몸짓으로   이렇게 멋지게 걷는 것은 습관적인 것이었다 /

and not for show, / for spectators were few.
보여주기 위한 것이 아니라 /   왜냐하면 구경하는 사람은 거의 없었기 때문에

The time was barely 10 o'clock at night, /
시각은 겨우 밤 10시였다 /

but chilly gusts of wind / with a little rain /
그러나 차갑게 부는 돌풍이 /   비가 조금씩 오면서 /

had almost depeopled the streets.
거리에 사람들이 거의 없도록 만들었다.

Trying doors / as he went, / twirling his club /
(문단속이 잘되어있는지) 문을 확인하고 / 그는 지나가면서 / 곤봉을 빙빙 돌리며 /

with many intricate and artful movements, / turning /
복잡하고 교묘한 동작으로 /   몸을 돌릴 때 /

now and then to cast his watchful eye down /
때때로 감시하듯이 눈초리를 보내려고 /

the pacific thoroughfare, / the officer, /
평화로운 도로에 / (이런 행동을 하는 동안에) 그 경찰관은 /

with his stalwart form and slight swagger, /
건장한 체격과 약간 뽐내며 걷고 있던 /

made a fine picture / of a guardian of the peace.
(그는) 멋진 모습이 되었다 /   평화의 수호자의

People in this part of the city / kept early hours.
도시에 이 지역에 사는 사람들은 /   일찍 자고 일찍 일어났다.

Now and then you might see / the lights of a cigar store /
종종 당신은 볼 수 있다 /   담배 가게의 불빛을 /

or of an all-night lunch counter; /
또는 24시간 영업하는 간이식당의 (불빛을)

but the majority of the doors belonged to business places /
그러나 대부분의 문은 사무소 건물에 속했다 /

that had been closed hours ago.
(그 건물들은) 오래전에 문을 닫았던

When about midway of a certain block /
어떤 구역의 중간쯤에 이르렀을 때 /

the policeman suddenly slowed / his walk.
경찰관은 갑자기 늦추었다 /   걸음걸이를

In the doorway of a darkened hardware store /
불이 꺼진 철물점의 현관에 /

a man leaned, / with an unlighted cigar in his mouth.
한 남자가 기대어 서있었다 / 불을 붙이지 않은 시가를 입에 문 채

As the policeman walked up / to him /
경찰관이 다가갔을 때 /   그 남자에게 /

the man spoke up quickly.
그 남자는 재빨리 말을 했다

"It's all right, officer," he said, reassuringly.
아무 것도 아닙니다 경찰관 나리   그가 안심시키듯이 말했다

"I'm just waiting for a friend.
저는 그냥 친구를 기다리고 있어요

It's an appointment / made twenty years ago."
약속이에요 /   20년 전에 했던

---

on the beat 담당 구역을 순회중인 avenue 가로수길 impressiveness 인상적임 spectator 구경꾼
chilly 냉랭한 depeople ~의 주민을 없애다 twirl 빙빙 돌리다 intricate 복잡한 artful 교묘한
watchful 감시하는 pacific 평화스러운 thoroughfare 도로 stalwart 건장한 slight 약간 swagger 뽐내며 걷기
picture 모습, 광경 guardian 수호자 majority 대부분 reassuringly 안심시키듯이

SCENE 2

"Sounds a little funny to you, / doesn't it?, said the man.
좀 이상한 이야기 같지요 / 안 그래요? 그 남자가 말했다

Well, I'll explain / if you'd like to make certain /
음, 제가 설명해드리죠 / 당신이 확실히 알고 싶으시다면 /

it's all straight.
제 말이 진짜인지

About that long ago there used to be a restaurant /
대략 그때쯤(약 20년 전에) 한 식당이 있었어요 /

where this store stands. 'Big Joe' Brady's restaurant."
(자리에) 이 가게가 있는 '빅 조' 브래디의 식당이라는 가게였죠

"Until five years ago," said the policeman.
5년 전까지만 해도 (있었죠) 경찰관이 말했다

"It was torn down then."
그 당시 철거됐습니다

The man in the doorway / struck a match and lit his cigar.
현관에 있던 그 남자는 / 성냥을 그었고 시가에 불을 붙였다

The light showed / a pale, square-jawed face /
성냥불이 보여주었다 / 창백하고 사각형의 턱이 있는 얼굴을 /

with keen eyes, / and a little white scar /
날카로운 눈매의 / 그리고 작은 하얀 상처를(보여주었다) /

near his right eyebrow.
오른쪽 눈썹 부근에 있는

His scarfpin was a large diamond, / oddly set.
그의 넥타이핀은 큰 다이아몬드였다 / 특이하게 새겨진

"Twenty years ago tonight," said the man, /
20년 전 오늘밤 그 남자가 말했다 /

"I dined here / at 'Big Joe' Brady's / with Jimmy Wells, /
저는 여기서 식사를 했죠 / '빅 조' 브래디라는 식당에서 / 지미 웰즈와 함께 /

my best chum, and the finest chap in the world.
제 가장 친구였고 / 세상에서 제일 좋은 놈이기도 했던

He and I grew up together / here in New York, /
그 친구와 저는 함께 자랐어요 / 여기 뉴욕에서 /

just like two brothers.
두 형제처럼

I was eighteen and Jimmy was twenty.
저는 18살이었고 지미는 20살이었죠

The next morning I was to start / for the West /
다음날 아침 저는 출발할 예정이었어요 / 서부로 /

to make my fortune.
(왜) 돈을 벌려고

You couldn't have dragged Jimmy /
당신일지라도 지미를 끌고 갈 수가 없었을 거예요 /

out of New York; / he thought /
뉴욕 밖으로 / 그는 생각하고 있었어요 /

it was the only place on earth.
뉴욕은 세상에서 (살 수 있는) 유일한 곳이라고

Well, we agreed that night /
어쨌든, 우리는 그날 밤 약속을 했어요 /

that we would meet here again / exactly twenty years /
(어떤 약속?) 우리가 여기서 다시 만나기로 / 정확히 20년 후에 /

from that date and time, / no matter what our conditions
같은 날과 시각에 / 어떤 상황일지라도

might be / or from what distance / we might have to come.
또는 얼마나 먼 거리에서 / 우리가 만나러 와야 하든지

We figured that / in twenty years each of us / would know /
우리는 생각했지요 / (뭐라고?)20년이 지나면 우리 각자가 / 알 것이라고 /

what kind of men we were, / and what future waited for us /
어떤 부류의 사람이 우리가 될지 / 어떤 미래가 우리를 기다리고 있는지 (알 것이라고)

and that / we would make our fortunes."
그리고 (생각했지요) / 우리는 큰 돈도 벌 것이라고

> ### Key Expression
>
> **"be to 부정사"가 어떤 의미로 쓰일지 결정하는 힌트는 문장 안에 있다.**
>
> be to 부정사는 "예정, 의무, 가능, 운명, 의도"와 같이 다양한 의미로 쓰인다. 예를 들어 아래에 나온 문장에는 "~할 예정이다"라는 의미로 쓰이는지 알아 볼 수 있는 힌트가 3가지가 있다. 첫째 "start(출발하다)"라는 동사, 둘째 어디를 향해떠나는지 여행의 목적지를 표시하는 "for", 셋째 언제 출발할 것인지 나타내는 "next morning"를 보면, 언제, 어떤 목적지를 향해떠날 예정이라는 것을 알 수 있다.
>
> The next morning I was to start / for the West / to make my fortune.
> 다음날 아침 저는 출발할 예정이었어요. / 서부로 / (왜) 돈을 벌려고

make certain ~을 확인하다 straight 신뢰할 수 있는 tear down (건물을) 해체하다, 철거하다
lit (light-lit-lit) 불을 붙이다 square-jawed 사각형의 턱을 가진 scar 흉터 dine 정찬을 먹다 chum 친구
chap 놈, 녀석 fortune 부, 재산 conditions 상황 distance 거리 figure ~라고 생각하다

SCENE 3

"It sounds pretty interesting," said the policeman.
아주 흥미로운데 / 경찰관이 말했다

"Rather a long time between meetings, / it seems to me.
만나기까지 꽤 긴 시간인 것 / 같군요

Haven't you heard / from your friend / since you left?"
소식을 들었나요 / 친구로부터 / 당신이 떠난 후에

"Well, yes, for a time we corresponded," said the other.
예 있어요. 한동안 연락을 했었죠 / 그 남자가 말했다

"But after a year or two we lost track of each other.
그러나 1~2년 후에 우리는 연락이 끊겼어요

You see, the West is pretty big, /
아시다시피, 서부는 아주 큰 지역이죠 /

and I kept moving around / everywhere pretty quickly.
그리고 저는 여기저기 돌아다녔어요 / 사방을 상당히 바쁘게

But I know / Jimmy will meet me here / if he's alive, /
그러나 나는 알아요 / 지미는 여기서 날 만날 것이라는 것을 / 지미가 살아있으면 /

for he always was the truest, / stanchest old chap /
왜냐하면 그 녀석은 언제나 진실하고 / 신뢰할 수 있는 오래된 친구이기 때문이에요 /

in the world. He'll never forget.
세상에서 / 그는 절대 까먹지 않을 거예요

I came a thousand miles / to stand in this door tonight, /
저는 1천 마일을 왔어요 / 오늘밤 이문 앞에 서 있으려고 /

and it's worth it / if my old partner turns up."
그리고 그럴 만한 가치가 있네요 / 만일 오랜 친구가 나타난다면

The waiting man pulled out / a handsome watch, /
기다리고 있던 남자가 꺼냈다 / 멋진 시계를

the lids of it set with small diamonds.
시계 뚜껑에는 작은 다이아몬드가 박혀있었다

"Three minutes to ten," he announced.
10시 3분전 / 그가 말했다

"It was exactly ten o'clock / when we parted here /
정확히 10시 정각이었죠 / 우리가 이곳에서 헤어졌을 때가 /

at the restaurant door."
식당 문에

"You were successful in the West, / weren't you?"
서부에서 성공했지요 / 그렇지 않아요?

asked the policeman.
경찰관이 물었다

"I surely was! I hope / Jimmy has done half / as well.
그럼요 저는 좋겠어요 / 지미가 절반만이라도 성공했으면 / 나와 마찬가지로

He was a kind of plodder, though, good fellow as he was.
그 친구는 꾸준히 일하는 사람이었어요, 하지만, 좋은 녀석이었어요

I've had to compete / with some of the sharpest wits /
저는 경쟁해야 했어요 / 아주 약삭빠른 놈들과 /

to make my fortune.
큰 재산을 모으기 위해서

A man gets in a groove / in New York.
사람이 고정된 생활 습관에 빠져요 / 뉴욕에 살면

In the West you learn / how to fight / for your success.
(그렇지만) 서부에서는 배울 수 있어요 / 경쟁하는 방법을 / 성공하려고

Key Expression 🔑

상황을 의미하는 "it"

"it"은 문맥상 파악할 수 있는 상황를 가리킬 때가 있다. 아래에 있는 예문을 보면 "it"은 "친구를 만나러 일천 마일을 여행한 상황"을 의미한다. 그래서 "It's worth it"을 직역해보면, "일천 마일 여행한 것은 그런 여행을 할만한 가치가 있다."라는 의미로 쓰였다.

I came a thousand miles / to stand in this door tonight, / and it's worth it / if my old partner turns up."
그럴 만한 가치가 있네요.

---

correspond 연락하다 lose track of 연락이 끊기다, (사람의 동향을) 알 수 없게 되다 stanch=staunch 믿음직한 turn up 나타나다 lid 뚜껑 announce 큰소리로 말하다 plodder 꾸준히 일하는 사람, 공부벌레 sharp 약삭빠른 wit 기지 있는 사람, 재주꾼 groove 고정적인 습관, 관례

SCENE 4

The policeman twirled / his club / and took a step or two.
경찰관은 빙빙 돌리며 / 곤봉을 / 그리고 한 두 걸음 걸어갔다

"I'll be on my way.
저는 그만 가봐야겠어요

Hope your friend comes around all right.
친구 분이 나타나길 바랍니다

Are you going to leave / if he isn't here / at ten sharp?
떠날 거예요 / 만일 친구 분이 오지 않으면 / 10시 정각에

"I should say not!" said the other.
아니 그렇지 않지요! 그 남자는 말했다

"I'll give him half an hour at least.
저는 최소한 30분을 더 기다릴 생각이에요

If Jimmy is alive on earth / he'll be here / by that time.
만약 지미가 세상에 살아있다면 / 그 친구는 여기에 올 거예요 / 그 시간까지

So long, officer."
안녕히 가세요, 경찰관 아저씨

"Good-night, sir," said the policeman, /
안녕히 가십시오 / 경찰관이 말했다 /

passing on along his beat, / trying doors / as he went.
(그리고) 순찰 구역을 따라 움직이면서 / 문단속을 했다 / 지나가면서

There was now a fine, cold drizzle falling, /
이제는 가늘고 차가운 이슬비가 내리고 있었다 /

and the wind got stronger, / so now it blew steadily.
그리고 바람은 더욱 거세졌고 / 이제는 바람이 지속적으로 불었다

The few pedestrians / in that quarter /
몇 명 안 되는 행인들이 / 그 지역에 돌아다니는 /

hurried dismally and silently along /
침울하고 조용히 걸음을 재촉했다 /

with coat collars turned high /
코트 깃을 세우고 /

and their hands in their pockets.
주머니에 손을 넣고

And in the door of the hardware store, /
그리고 철물점 현관에서 /

the man / who had come a thousand miles / to keep an
그 남자는 /　　(어떤 남자?) 1천 마일을 왔던 /

appointment / with the friend of his youth, /
약속을 지키기 위해서 / 젊은 시절의 친구와 /

smoked his cigar and waited.
시가에 불을 붙이고 기다렸다.

Such a meeting could be uncertain / almost to absurdity.
이런 식으로 만나는 것은 불확실한 것일 것이다 /　　어리석을 정도로

About twenty minutes he waited, /
약 20분쯤 그는 기다렸다 /

and then a tall man in a long overcoat, /
그리고 나서 긴 코트를 입은 키가 큰 남자가 /

with collar turned up to his ears, / hurried across /
칼라를 귀까지 세우고 /　　　　　　　　급하게 왔다 /

from the opposite side of the street.
거리의 반대편으로부터

He went directly / to the waiting man.
그 남자는 곧바로 갔다 /　기다리고 있는 남자에게로

Key Expression

"with +목적어 +분사"는 주어와 술어관계를 표현한다.

"with +목적어 +분사"가 있는 문장에는 두개의 사건을 표현한다. 보통 첫 번째 사건이 표현되고, 그 다음에 "with"를 이용하여 그 사건과 동시에 일어나는 또 다른 사건을 설명한다. 그래서 "~한 채로", "~하면서"라고 해석한다. 목적어 다음에 오는 분사는 현재분사, 과거분사, 형용사, 전치사구, 부사가 올 수 있다. 목적어 다음에 어떤 표현이 오든 목적어와 분사는 주어와 술어관계(~이 ~하면서, ~이 ~한 채로)로 보면, 쉽게 이해할 수 있다.

The pedestrians / hurried home /
행인들이 / 서둘러 귀가했다 /
with coat collars turned high / and their hands in their pockets.
(어떻게?) 코트 깃이 높이 세워졌고 / 손이 주머니에 있는 채로

come around 나타나다　sharp 정각에　beat 순찰 구역　fine 가느다란　drizzle 이슬비　steadily 지속적으로
pedestrian 행인　quarter 지역　dismally 침울하게　absurdity 어리석은 일　opposite 정반대의

SCENE 5

"Is that you, Bob?" he asked, / doubtfully.
밥이니? 그가 물었다 / 의심스러운 듯이

"Is that you, Jimmy Wells?" cried the man in the door.
지미 웰즈니? 현관에 있던 남자가 외쳤다

The new arrival / grasped both the other's hands /
새로 온 남자는 / 상대방의 두 손을 붙잡았다 /

with his own.
자신의 손으로

"It's Bob, / sure as fate. I was certain / I'd find you here /
밥이야 / 틀림없이 나는 확신했어어 / 여기서 너를 만날 줄 /

if you were still in existence.
네가 여전히 살아있다면

Well, well, well! -twenty years is a long time.
그럼, 그럼, 그럼! 20년은 긴 세월이지

The old restaurant's gone, Bob; / I wish / it had lasted, /
옛날의 식당은 사라졌어, 밥 / 난 바랬는데 / 식당이 계속 있어주길 /

so we could have had / another dinner there.
(식당이 있었다면) 우리가 먹을 수 있었을 텐데 / 저녁을 다시 한 번

How has the West treated you, / old man?"
서부에서는 어땠어 / 친구야

"Incredible; it has given me everything / I asked it for.
엄청나지. 서부는 나에게 모든 것을 주었지(뭐든지 가질 수가 있지) / 내가 원하는

You've changed lots, Jimmy.
넌 많이 변했구나, 지미.

I never thought / you were so tall."
난 몰랐는걸 / 네가 그렇게 클 줄

"Oh, I grew a bit / after I was twenty."
오, 나는 좀 컸어 / 20세가 넘어서

"Doing well in New York, Jimmy?"
뉴욕에서 잘 지내, 지미

"Moderately. I have a position /
그냥 그래 근무하고 있어 /

in one of the city departments.
시청의 한 부서에서

Come on, Bob; / we'll go around / to a place I know of, /
자, 밥 / 가자 / 내가 아는 곳으로 /

and have a good long talk / about old times."
그리고 실컷 이야기하자 / 옛 시절에 대해서

The two men started up the street, / arm in arm.
두 남자는 거리를 걷기 시작했다 / 팔짱을 끼고

The man from the West, /
서부에서 온 남자는 /

his egotism enlarged by success, /
자만심이 성공에 의해 부풀어서 /

was beginning to tell / the story of his career.
이야기하기 시작했다 / 자신의 성공담을

The other, / submerged in his overcoat, /
키 큰 남자는 / 오버코트에 파묻혀서 /

listened with interest. At the corner / stood a drug store, /
흥미롭게 귀 기울였다 코너에 / 약국이 하나 있었다 /

brilliant with electric lights.
전등불로 환하게 빛나는

When they came into this glare /
두 남자가 그 불빛 안으로 들어오자 /

each of them turned simultaneously /
두 사람 각자는 동시에 몸을 돌렸다 /

to gaze upon the other's face.
서로의 얼굴을 응시하려고

Key Expression

have +a +명사를 보면, 명사를 동사처럼 해석한다.

회화할 때 자주 사용되며, 1회 한정된 동작을 표현한다.

have a talk 이야기하다
have a bath 목욕하다
have a swim 수영하다
have a walk 산책하다
have a try 한번 해보다
have a chat 잡담하다

in existence 생존하고 있는 treat 대우하다, 대접하다 incredible 믿을 수 없는 moderately 적당히 egotism 자만 enlarge 커지다 career 성공, 출세 submerged 파묻혀서, 몰두해서 glare 불빛 simultaneously 동시에 gaze 응시하다

SCENE 6

The man from the West stopped suddenly /
서부에서 온 남자는 갑자기 멈췄고 /

and released his arm.
팔짱을 끼었던 팔을 풀었다

"You're not Jimmy Wells," he snapped.
당신은 지미 웰즈가 아니잖아   그가 날카롭게 말했다

"Twenty years is a long time, / but not long /
20년은 긴 세월이야 /   그러나 긴 세월은 아냐 /

enough to change a man's nose / from a Roman to a pug."
사람의 코를 변화시킬 만큼 /   오똑한 코를 돼지코로

"It sometimes changes / a good man into a bad one, /
그것(20년이라는 세월)은 때때로 변화시키지 / 좋은 사람을 나쁜 사람으로 /

said the tall man.
키 큰 남자가 말했다

"You've been under arrest / for ten minutes, Bob.
너는 체포되었어 /   10분 동안, 밥

The Chicago cops thought / you would come to New York.
시카고 경찰은 생각했어 /   네가 뉴욕에 올 것이라고 /

They told us / to watch for you.
그들이 말했지 /   너를 감시하라고

They want to have a chat / with you.
그들은 너와 말하길 원해 /   너와

Are you coming with me / quietly?
나를 따라올 거지 /   순순히

That's sensible.
그것 참 현명하군

Now, before we go on to the police station /
이제 경찰서로 가기 전에 /

here's a note / I was asked to hand to you.
쪽지가 있어 /   너에게 전해주라고 부탁받은

You may read it / here at the window.
읽어봐 /   여기 창가에서

It's from Patrolman Wells."
순찰경관인 웰즈가 보낸 것이야

60   O. Henry's Short Stories

The man from the West unfolded /
서부에서 온 남자는 폈다 /

the little piece of paper / handed him.
조그맣게 접은 종이를 그에게 /   건네주었던

His hand was steady / when he began to read, /
그의 손은 침착했다 /   그가 읽기 시작했을 때 /

but it trembled / a little / by the time he had finished.
그러나 손이 떨렸다 / 조금 / 그가 다 읽었을 때

The note was rather short.
쪽지는 짧은 편이었다

"Bob: I was at the appointed place / on time.
밥, 나는 약속한 장소에 있었어 /   시간에 맞춰

When you struck the match / to light your cigar /
네가 성냥불을 그었을 때 /   시가에 불을 붙이려고 /

I saw / it was the face of the man wanted in Chicago.
나는 알았지 / 그것(불에 비친 얼굴)이 시카고에서 현상수배를 받고 있는 자의 얼굴이었다는 것을

Somehow I couldn't do it myself, / so I went around /
아무튼 나는 체포할 수 없었어 /   그래서 나는 돌아가서 /

and got / a plain clothes man to do the job.
(~하도록) 설득했지 / 사복 경찰관이 너를 체포하도록

JIMMY."
지미

Key Expression

"be asked"는 누군가의 "부탁이나 요청을 받다"라고 해석한다.

I was asked to help her.
나는 부탁을 받았다 / 그녀를 도와주라고
I was asked to explain how to make the final decision.
나는 부탁을 받았다 / 설명해달라는 / 어떻게 내가 최종결정을 내리는지
I was asked to pass along this message.
나는 부탁을 받았다 / 이 메시지를 전달해 달라는

---

release 풀어놓다 snap 날카롭게 말하다, 호통 치듯이 말하다 Roman nose 서양 사람들의 긴 코
pug nose 넓고 짧은 코 under arrest 체포되다 chat 잡담 sensible 현명한 patrolman 순찰경관 unfold 펴다
wanted 수배중인 get 권유해서 ~시키다, plain clothes man 사복 경찰관

Quiz 3

A. 내용 이해하기

다음 문장을 읽고 본문의 내용과 맞으면 T(True), 틀리면 F(False)를 쓰세요.

1. 20 years ago Jimmy and Bob made a promise to meet again at the place where they had dined and parted.
2. The policeman was not interested in what Jimmy's talking about.
3. Jimmy made a big fortune in the West.
4. Actually, the patrolman was Bob and Jimmy didn't recognized him at the first sight.

B. 단어

다음 제시된 단어의 설명을 읽고, 어떤 단어의 정의를 설명하는지 아래의 박스에서 찾아 써 보세요.

1. to let a person go free after he has been kept somewhere
2. a person who guards or protects someone
3. a permanent mark left on your skin after a wound has healed
4. having many complexly arranged elements
5. one who is walking along a street
6. having physical strength
7. someone who is watching an event
8. done in a clever and attracting way; skillful
9. something to be done in the same way for a long time; a settled routine
10. a state of being; the situation in which something exists
11. to turn around and around
12. peaceful and loving peace
13. honest and truthful

> spectator twirl intricate artful pacific stalwart guardian
> straight scar condition groove pedestrian release

Answer

A. 1. T 2. F 3. F 4. T

B. 1. release 2. guardian 3. scar 4. intricate 5. pedestrian 6. stalwart 7. spectator 8. artful 9. groove 10. condition 11. twirl 12. pacific 13. straight

C. 직독직해

아래에 제시된 문장을 직독직해로 해석해보세요.

1. In the doorway of a darkened hardware store / a man leaned, / with an unlighted cigar in his mouth.

    →

2. We agreed that night / that we would meet here again / exactly twenty years / from that date and time, / no matter what our conditions might be.

    →

3. The few pedestrians / hurried dismally and silently along / with coat collars turned high and their hands in their pockets.

    →

4. Twenty years is a long time, / but not long / enough to change a man's nose / from a Roman to a pug.

    →

D. 동시통역

아래에 제시된 직독직해를 보고, 영어로 말해보세요.

1. 순찰중인 경찰관 한명이 / 거리를 따라 걸었다 / 인상적인 몸짓으로

    →

2. 제가 설명해드리죠 / 당신이 확실히 알고 싶으시다면 / 제 말이 진짜인지

    →

3. 서부에서 온 남자는 갑자기 멈췄고 / 팔짱을 끼었던 팔을 풀었다.

    →

4. 나는 약속한 장소에 있었다. / 시간에 맞춰

    →

Answer

C. 1. 불이 꺼진 철물점의 현관에 / 한 남자가 기대어 서있었다 / 불을 붙이지 않은 시가를 입에 문 채 2. 우리는 그날 밤 약속을 했어요 / (어떤 약속?) 우리가 여기서 다시 만나기로 / 정확히 20년 후에 / 같은 날과 시각에 / 어떤 상황일지라도 3. 몇 명 안 되는 행인들이 / 침울하고 조용히 걸음을 재촉했다 / 코트 깃을 세우고 주머니에 손을 넣고 4. 20년은 긴 세월이야 / 그러나 긴 세월은 아냐 / 사람의 코를 변화시킬 만큼 / 오뚝한 코를 돼지코로

D. 1. The policeman on the beat / moved up the avenue / impressively. 2. I'll explain / if you'd like to make certain / it's all straight. 3. The man from the West stopped suddenly / and released his arm. 4. I was at the appointed place / on time.

The Gift of the Magi
현자의 선물

SCENE 1

One dollar and eighty-seven cents.
1불 87센트

That was all. And sixty cents of it was in pennies.
이게 전부였다   게다가 그 중에서 60센트는 1센트짜리 동전이었다

Pennies saved one and two / at a time /
이 동전들은 한 두 개씩 모였다 /   한 번에 /

by bulldozing / the grocer and the vegetable man and the
(어떻게?) 억지를 써서 / 식료품 장수, 야채장수, 정육점주인에게 /

butcher / until one's cheeks burned /
        (언제까지?) 얼굴이 화끈거릴 때까지 /

with the silent condemnation of being stingy /
말은 안하지만 인색하다는 비난으로 /

that such close dealing accompanies.
(어떤 비난?) 그렇게 아슬아슬한 흥정에 따르는

Three times Della counted it.
세 번 델라는 돈을 세어보았다

One dollar and eighty-seven cents.
1불 87센트

And the next day would be Christmas.
그리고 내일은 크리스마스다

There was clearly nothing to do /
분명히 할 일은 없었다 /

but flop down on / the shabby little couch / and cry.
(제외하곤) 주저앉아서 / 초라하고 작은 소파에 /   우는 것을 (제외하곤)

So Della did it. That leads to / the moral reflection /
델라는 그렇게 했다(울었다) 그런 것(주저앉아 우는 것)은 하게한다 / 도덕적인 반성을 /

that life is made up of / sobs, sniffles, and smiles, /
(도덕적 반성이란?) 인생은 이뤄져 있다는 / 흐느낌, 코를 훌쩍거림 그리고 미소로 /

with sniffles predominating.
코를 훌쩍거리는 것이 압도적이지만

While the mistress of the home is gradually subsiding /
여주인이 서서히 마음이 진정되는 동안 /

from the first stage to the second, /
(울부짖는) 첫 번째 단계에서 (훌쩍거리는) 두 번째 단계로 /

take a look at the home.
집을 한번 보자

A furnished flat / at $8 per week.
가구가 딸린 아파트 방으로 / 1주일에 8불짜리

It was not exactly beyond description, /
아파트 방은 반드시 묘사할 수 없는 것은 아니다

but it certainly / had to be on the lookout /
(묘사할 수 없을 정도로 형편없는 것은 아니지만) / 그러나 그 방은 분명히 / 경계해야 했다 /

for a crowd of beggars.
거지 집단이 몰려오는 것을 (거지들이 살 정도로 매우 초라한 아파트 방이었다)

In the hall below was a letter-box / into which /
아래층 입구에는 우편함이 하나가 있었다 / 그 편지함으로 /

no letter would go, / and an electric bell / from which /
어떤 편지도 들어가지 않는 / 그리고 전기초인종이 있었다 / 그리고 그 초인종으론 /

no mortal finger could ring.
어떤 인간의 손도 울리게 할 수 없는

Also beside the door / was a card /
또한 문 옆에 있었다 / 문패가 하나가 /

bearing the name "Mr. James Dillingham Young."
'제임스 딜링햄 영' 이라는 이름이 있는

Key Expression

"but" 에는 "~을 제외하고" 라는 의미도 있다.

She did nothing but howl.
그녀는 아무것도 하지 않았다 / 울부짖는 것을 제외하고(그녀는 울부짖을 뿐이었다)
What can I do but sit and wait?
무엇을 할 수 있을까 / 앉아서 기다리는 것(관망하는 것)을 제외하고
I have no choice but to accept his offer.
다른 선택은 없다 / 받아들이는 것을 제외하고(받아들일 수밖에 없다) / 그의 제안을

bulldoze 협박하다, 강행하다 butcher 정육점 주인 condemnation 비난 stingy 인색한 close 아슬아슬한 accompany ~와 함께 있다, 동반하다 shabby 초라한 sniffle 코를 훌쩍거림 predominating 압도적인 mistress 여주인 gradually 차츰, 서서히, 점진적으로 subside 가라앉다 furnished flat 가구가 갖춰진 아파트 not exactly 반드시 ~하지 않다, 반드시 ~는 아니다 lookout 경계 mortal 인간의 bear (명성, 칭호 등을) 가지다

SCENE 2

The "Dillingham" had been flung to the breeze /
'딜링햄' 이란 이름이 산들바람에 기세 좋게 움직였다 /

during a former period of prosperity /
예전에 번영할 시기에는

when its possessor was being paid / $30 per week.
(언제?) 그 이름의 주인이 받고 있을 때 /   1주일에 30달러를

Now, when the income was shrunk / to $20, /
이제는 수입이 1주일에 줄어들었던 시기인 / 20달러로 /

the letters of "Dillingham" looked blurred, /
'딜링햄' 이란 글자가 희미하게 보였다 /

as though they were thinking seriously /
마치 글자들이 진지하게 생각하는 것처럼 /

of contracting to a modest and unassuming D.
겸손하고 건방지지 않는 대문자 D로 많이 줄어드는 것을

But whenever Mr. James Dillingham Young came home /
그러나 (~할 때마다) 제임스 딜링햄 영이 집에 와서

and reached his flat above / he was called "Jim" /
2층으로 올라왔을 (때마다) /   그는 '짐' 이라고 불렸고 /

and greatly hugged / by Mrs. James Dillingham Young, /
따스하게 포옹을 받았다 /   제임스 딜링햄 영부인에 의해 /

already introduced / to you / as Della.
이미 소개된 /   독자 여러분께 / '델라' 라고

That is all very good.
그것은 매우 흐뭇한 광경이다

Della finished her cry / and attended to her cheeks /
델라는 울음을 그치고 /   뺨을 두드렸다 /

with the powder rag.
분첩으로

She stood by the window / and looked out dully /
그녀는 창가에 서서 /   그리고 무심히 바라보았다 /

at a grey cat / walking a grey fence /
회색 고양이를 /   (어떤 고양이?) 회색 울타리를 걷고 있는 /

in a grey backyard.
회색 뒷마당에서

Tomorrow would be Christmas Day, /
내일은 크리스마스다 /

and she had only $1.87 / with which /
그리고 그녀는 겨우 1불 87센트밖에 없었다 / 그 돈으로 /

to buy Jim a present.
짐에게 선물을 사줄 수 있는

She had been saving / every penny /
그녀는 모았다 / 모든 동전을 /

she could for months, / with this result.
수개월 동안 그녀가 모을 수 있는 / 결과는 이렇다

Twenty dollars a week / doesn't go far.
1주일에 20불이라는 수입으로는 / (큰 돈을 모으는데) 도움이 되지 않는다

Expenses had been greater / than she had calculated.
지출이 훨씬 많았다 / 그녀가 계산했던 것보다

They always are.
언제나 그렇다

Only $1.87 / to buy a present for Jim. Her Jim.
겨우 1불 87센트만 있다 / 짐에게 선물 사줄 돈은 / 그녀의 짐을 위해서

Many a happy hour / she had spent /
행복한 많은 시간을 / 그녀는 보냈다 /

planning for something nice / for him.
뭔가 멋진 것을 계획하느라 / 짐을 위해서

Something fine and rare and excellent /
뭔가 근사하고 귀하고 훌륭한 것 /

-something just a little bit near /
좀더 가까운 것 /

to being worthy of the honor of being owned by Jim.
짐이 소유했다고 자랑할만한 것에

---

fling (fling-flung-flung) 기세 좋게 움직이다 breeze 산들바람 prosperity 번영, 유복 possessor 소유자, 주인 shrink (shrink-shrunk-shrunk) 줄어들다 blurred 희미한, 흐릿한 contract 줄어들다 unassuming 겸손한 attend 보살피다 go far 도움이 되다 expense 지출 calculate 계산하다 worthy ~할만한, 어울리는 honor 자랑, 특권

SCENE 3

There was a pier-glass / between the windows of the room.
큰 거울이 있었다 / 그 방의 창문과 창문 사이에는

Perhaps you have seen / a pier-glass in an $8 flat.
아마 당신도 본 적이 있을 것이다 / 8불짜리 아파트에 있는 큰 거울을

A very thin and very agile person may, /
아주 마르고 아주 머리 회전이 빠른 사람이라면 /

by observing his reflection /
(어떻게?) 거울에 비친 모습을 보고서 /

in a rapid sequence of longitudinal strips, /
잇달아 빠르게 가는 수직 조각으로 (비춰진) /

obtain a fairly accurate conception / of his looks.
(상당히 정확한 이해를 얻을 수 있다) 매우 정확하게 이해할 수 있다 / 자신의 (실제) 모습을

Della, / being slender, / had mastered the art.
델라는 / 마른 / 그 요령을 숙달했다

Suddenly she whirled from the window /
갑자기 그녀는 창가에서 몸을 돌리고 /

and stood before the glass.
거울 앞에 섰다

Her eyes were shining brilliantly, /
그녀의 눈이 찬란히 빛나고 있었다 /

but her face had lost its color / within twenty seconds.
그러나 그녀의 얼굴은 창백해졌다 / 20초 만에

Rapidly she pulled down her hair / and let it fall /
재빨리 그녀는 머리를 풀어서 / 늘어뜨렸다 /

to its full length. Now, there were two possessions /
원래 길이대로 그런데 2개의 소유물이 있었다 /

of the James Dillingham Youngs /
제임스 딜링햄 영 부부에게는 /

in which they both took a mighty pride.
그 물건을 두 사람은 아주 자랑스럽게 여겼던

One was Jim's gold watch /
하나는 짐의 금시계였다 /

that had been his father's and his grandfather's.
(그 시계는) 그의 아버지와 할아버지의 소유물이었던

The other was Della's hair.
또 하나는 델라의 머리카락이었다

Had a queen lived / in the flat near theirs, /
만일 여왕이 살았었더라면 /   그들의 아파트 근처에 /

Della would have let her hair hang out the window /
델라는 머리를 창문 밖으로 늘어뜨리면 /

some day to dry / just to depreciate /
언젠가 머리를 말리기 위해서 / (그러면) 결국 가치를 떨어뜨릴 뿐이다 /

Her Majesty's jewels and gifts.
여왕의 보석과 선물의

Had King Solomon been the janitor, /
솔로몬 왕이 관리인이었다면 /

with all his treasures piled up in the basement, /
(어떤 관리인?) 그의 보물이 지하에 쌓여 있는 /

Jim would have pulled out his watch /
짐은 시계를 꺼냈을 것이다 /

every time he passed, /
(관리인인) 솔로몬 왕이 지나갈 때마다 /

just to see / him pluck at his beard / from envy.
(왜?) 단지 보려고 / 솔로몬 왕이 자신의 수염을 쥐어뜯는 것을 / 부러워서

pier-glass 큰 거울 agile 머리 회전이 빠른 reflection (거울 속에) 비친 모습, 반성 sequence 연속, 결과
a sequence of 잇달아, 연속되는 longitudinal 수직의 conception (전체적인) 이해, 개념 whirl 돌다, 회전하다
possession 소유물 mighty 상당한, 대단한 depreciate 가치를 떨어뜨리다 pluck 잡아 뜯다 envy 질투, 시기

SCENE 4

So now Della's beautiful hair fell / about her, /
지금 델라의 아름다운 머리카락은 흘러내렸다 / 몸 주위에 /

rippling and shining / like a cascade of brown waters.
(그리고)잔잔하게 물결치고 반짝이였다 / 물결이 갈색인 폭포수처럼

It reached below her knee /
그것(머리카락)은 무릎 아래까지 늘어뜨려졌고 /

and made itself almost a garment for her.
거의 긴 옷처럼 되었다

And then she did it up / again nervously and quickly.
그리고 나서 그녀는 머리를 땋아 올렸다 / 다시 신경질적으로 재빨리

Once she faltered for a minute / and stood still /
잠시 망설였고 / 다음에 가만히 서있었다 /

while a tear or two splashed / on the worn red carpet.
(언제?) 눈물이 한 방울 두 방울 떨어졌다 / 낡은 붉은 카펫에

She put on her old brown jacket; /
낡은 갈색 자켓을 입었다 /

she put on her old brown hat. With a whirl of skirts /
그리고 그녀는 낡은 갈색 모자를 썼다. 치마를 펄럭이며 돌았고 /

and with the brilliant sparkle still in her eyes, /
반짝이는 눈물이 아직도 눈에 고인채로 /

she fluttered out the door / and down the stairs to the street.
그녀는 문밖으로 빠르게 나가고 / 계단을 내려와 거리로 (나갔다)

Where she stopped / the sign read: /
그녀가 멈춘 자리에서 / 간판에 적혀있었다 / (다음과 같이)

"Mme. Sofronie. Hair Goods of All Kinds."
음, 소프로니. 모든 종류의 머리 용품

One flight up Della ran, / and collected herself, / panting.
한 층의 계단을 뛰어 올라갔다 / 그리고 자신을 진정시켰다 / 숨을 헐떡이며

Madame, / large, too white, chilly, /
주인 여자는 / 덩치가 크고, 아주 하얗고, 창백한 /

hardly looked the "Sofronie."
'소프로니' 라는 이름에 어울리지 않아 보였다

"Will you buy my hair?" asked Della.
제 머리를 사실래요? 델라가 물어봤다

"I buy hair," said Madame.
사지요   주인 여자가 말했다

"Take your hat off / and let's have a sight /
모자를 벗고 /   보여주세요 /

at the looks of it."
머리채의 모습을

Down rippled / the brown cascade.
잔잔히 굽이치며 흘러내렸다 / 갈색 폭포수가

"Twenty dollars," said Madame, /
20달러   주인 여자가 말했다 /

lifting the mass / with a practiced hand.
머리채를 들어올리면서 /   능숙하게

"Give it to me quick," said Della.
얼른 20달러 주세요   델라가 말했다

Oh, and the next two hours tripped by / on rosy wings.
아, 그리고 그 후 2시간은 경쾌하게 지나갔다 /   장밋빛 날개를 달고

Forget / the hashed metaphor.
잊어주길 바란다 / 엉망으로 만들어진 비유(장밋빛 날개를 달고 움직이는 모습)를

She was ransacking the stores / for Jim's present.
그녀는 상점을 샅샅이 뒤졌다 /   짐에게 줄 선물을 사기 위해

Key Expression

영어의 논리란?

1) The sign reads; 간판에 ~라고 쓰여 있다.

간판을 읽고 이해하는 것은 사람이다. 그래서 사람들은 어떤 간판인지 읽고 이해할 수 있다. 하지만 간판의 입장에서 보면, 간판이 읽는 행위를 하는 것은 아니라 상호명이 쓰여 있을 뿐이다. 그래서 "read"는 "라고 쓰여 있다"라는 의미로 해석한다.

2) "동사+부사" 형태의 표현 중에 동사와 부사의 의미가 살아있는 것들이 있다. 이런 표현을 무조건 숙어처럼 익힐 필요가 없다.

flutter(빠르게 움직이다) +out(밖으로) = 빠르게 밖으로 나가다
trip(경쾌하게 움직이다) +by(~의 곁을) = 경쾌하게 지나가다

"flutter out"에 있는 flutter(날갯짓하며 날다; 빠르게 움직이다)를 보고, 새, 나비, 별이 날 때 날개를 빠르게 움직인다. 그래서 빠르게 움직인다는 의미로 사용된 것을 유추할 수 있다. 그리고 부사(out)의 의미와 연결한다.

---

ripple 잔물결을 일으키다 cascade 작은 폭포 garment 의복, 옷 do up (머리를) 올리다
falter 머뭇거리다, 비틀거리다 splash 물속으로 풍덩하고 떨어지다 whirl 선회, 회전, 빙빙 돌기
sparkle 불꽃, 번쩍임 flutter 날갯짓하며 날다(빠르게 움직이다) flutter out 빠르게 나가다 flight 한 층의 계단
collect oneself 자신을 진정시키다(가다듬다) pant 숨을 헐떡이다 trip 경쾌하게 움직이다 trip by 경쾌하게 지나가다
hash 엉망으로 만들다 metaphor 비유 hashed metaphor 엉망으로 만들어진 비유 ransack 샅샅이 뒤지다

SCENE 5

She found / a gift for Jim / at last.
그녀는 찾아냈다 / 짐에게 줄 선물을 / 마침내

It surely had been made / for Jim / and no one else.
그것은 분명히 바로 안성맞춤인 것이었다 / 짐에게 / 하지만 다른 사람에겐 어울리지 않는

There was no other like it / in any of the stores, /
그와 같은 것은 없었다 / 다른 어떤 가게에도 /

and she had looked in every store / in the city.
그리고 그녀는 가게를 다 뒤져보았다 / 도시에 있는

It was a gold watch chain / simple and chaste in design, /
그것은 금 시곗줄이었고 / 디자인이 간단하고 품위 있었다 /

properly proclaiming / its value / by substance alone /
(그리고) 적절하게 드러냈다 / 시계의 가치를 / 금이라는 자체로만으로 /

and not by flashy ornamentation / - as all good things should
그리고 겉만 번지르르한 장식에 의해서가 아니라 / 좋은 물건들이 당연히 그러하듯이

do. It was even worthy of The Watch.
그것은 게다가 짐의 금시계에 어울렸다

As soon as she saw it / she knew / that it must be Jim's.
그녀는 그것을 보자마자 / 그녀는 알았다 / 그것이 짐의 것이 되어야 한다는 것을

It was like him. Quietness and value -the description applied /
그것은 그와 닮았다(그에게 어울렸다). 고요함과 가치 - 이 묘사가 적용되었다(어울렸다) /

to both. Twenty-one dollars they took / from her / for it, /
양쪽 모두에게. 21달러를 받았다 / 그녀로부터 / 물건값으로 /

and she hurried home / with the 87 cents.
그리고 그녀는 서둘러 집으로 돌아왔다 / 나머지 87센트를 갖고

With that chain on his watch /
그 시곗줄이 시계에 달려있으면 /

Jim could look at his watch / and learn the time /
짐은 시계를 보고 / 시간을 알 수 있을 것이다 /

in any company. Grand as the watch was, /
누구 앞에서도 시계가 멋졌지만 /

he sometimes looked at / it on the sly / on account of
짐은 때때로 보았다 / 시계를 남몰래 살짝 / 낡은 가죽 끈 때문에 /

the old leather strap / that he used in place of a chain.
(어떤 가죽 끈을?) 그가 시곗줄 대신에 쓰는

72   O. Henry's Short Stories

When Della reached home /
델라가 집에 왔을 때 /

her intoxication gave way a little / to prudence and reason.
그녀가 흥분되어 있던 마음은 차츰 변했다 / 신중하고 이성적이 상태로

She got out her curling irons / and lighted the gas /
그녀는 머리를 컬하는 고대기를 꺼내서 / 가스에 불을 붙였다 /

and went to work repairing / the ravages /
그리고 손질하기 시작했다 / 손상(손상된 머리)을 /

made by generosity added to love.
(남편에 대한) 사랑과 관용 때문에 생긴

That is always a tremendous task, dear friends /
그것은 언제나 엄청난 작업이다 /

-a mammoth task. Within forty minutes /
진짜 엄청난 작업이다 40분 이내에 /

her head was covered / with tiny, close-lying curls /
그녀의 머리는 덮어졌다 / 작은 달라붙은 곱슬머리로 /

that made her look / wonderfully like a truant schoolboy.
(이런 곱슬머리는) 그녀가 보이게 했다 / 놀랄 정도로 무단결석하는 남학생처럼

She looked at her reflection / in the mirror long and carefully.
그녀는 자신의 모습을 보았다 / 거울에서 찬찬히, 조심스럽게

Key Expression

"should" 의 여러 의미를 상황에 맞게 해석한다.

1. 의무를 표현할 때
   You shouldn't tell him about this. 너는 말하면 안 된다 / 그에게 이것에 대해

2. 주관적 판단, 감정을 표현할 때
   It is natural that you should be angry with me.
   당연하다 / (무엇이?) 네가 화난 것은 / 나에게

3. "should"는 말하는 사람의 "당연한 추측이나 기대"를 표현할 때
   – as all good things should do. 좋은 물건들이 당연히 그러하듯이.
   It should be very hot in summer there. 매우 무더운 것은 당연해 / 여름에 그곳은

4. 요구, 주장, 제안를 나타내는 문장의 "that"절 안에
   They insisted that the manager should resign.
   그들은 주장했다 / 매니저가 사임해야 된다고

chaste 품위 있는 proclaim 확실하게 나타내다, 보여주다 flashy 겉만 번지르르한 ornamentation 장식
worthy ~에 어울리는 apply 적합하다, 적용되다 grand 멋진, 훌륭한 on the sly 남몰래 살짝
on account of ~ 때문에 in place of ~대신에 intoxication 흥분, 도취 give way to 바뀌다, 변하다
prudence 신중함, 분별력 curling irons 컬을 만드는 고대기 ravage 손상, 파괴 generosity 관용
tremendous 엄청난 mammoth 거대한 curls 곱슬머리 truant 무단결석의

Quiz 4

A. 내용 이해하기

다음 문장을 읽고 본문의 내용과 맞으면 T(True), 틀리면 F(False)를 쓰세요.

1. Della wanted to buy a Christmas present for her beloved husband, Jim.
2. She went to Madame Sofronie's hair goods shop, where she sold her hair for a hundred bucks.
3. Della wore her naturally curly hair in order to make her look younger.
4. Della bought a gold watch for Jim.

B. 단어

다음 제시된 단어의 설명을 읽고, 어떤 단어의 정의를 설명하는지 아래의 박스에서 찾아 써 보세요.

1. willingness to give
2. an image that you can see in a mirror
3. to search thoroughly
4. decorations or the use of objects to decorate something
5. the feeling of wanting something that someone else has
6. very intelligent and mentally alert
7. not generous with money or spending reluctantly
8. something that you are very proud to do
9. being excited and unable to think clearly as a result of love
10. to pull out hairs with your fingers
11. an article of clothing
12. an expression of very strong disapproval of someone morally wrong
13. being sensible and careful when you make decisions

---

condemnation stingy honor agile reflection pluck envy garment
ransack prudence ornamentation intoxication generosity

Answer
A. 1. T 2. F 3. F 4. F
B. 1. generosity 2. reflection 3. ransack 4. ornamentation 5. envy 6. agile 7. stingy 8. honor
9. intoxication 10. pluck 11. garment 12. condemnation 13. prudence

C. 직독직해

아래에 제시된 문장을 직독직해로 해석해보세요.

1. Pennies saved one and two / at a time / by bulldozing / the grocer and the vegetable man and the butcher / until one's cheeks burned / with the silent condemnation of being stingy / that such close dealing accompanies.

   →

2. That leads to / the moral reflection / that life is made up of / sobs, sniffles, and smiles, / with sniffles predominating.

   →

3. In the hall below was a letter-box / into which / no letter would go, / and an electric bell / from which / no mortal finger could ring.

   →

D. 동시통역

아래에 제시된 직독직해를 보고, 영어로 말해보세요.

1. 지출이 훨씬 많았다 / 그녀가 계산했던 것보다

   →

2. 재빨리 그녀는 머리를 풀어서 / 늘어뜨렸다 / 원래 길이대로

   →

3. 그것은 분명히 바로 안성맞춤인 것이었다 / 짐에게 / 하지만 다른 사람에겐 어울리지 않는 것이었다

   →

4. 그녀는 그것을 보자마자 / 그녀는 알았다 / 그것이 짐의 것이 되어야 한다는 것을

   →

Answer

C. 1. 이 동전들은 한 두 개씩 모였다 / 한 번에 / (어떻게?) 억지를 써서 / 식료품 장수, 야채장수, 정육점주인에게 / (언제까지?) 얼굴이 화끈거릴 때까지 / 말은 안하지만 인색하다는 비난으로 / (어떤 비난?) 그렇게 아슬아슬한 흥정에 따르는 2. 이런 것(주저앉아 우는 것)은 하게한다. / 도덕적인 반성을 / (도덕적 반성이란?) 인생은 이뤄져 있다는 / 흐느낌, 코를 훌쩍거림 그리고 미소로 / 코를 훌쩍이며 우는 것이 압도적이지만 3. 아래층 입구에는 우편함이 하나가 있었다 / 그 편지함으로 / 어떤 편지도 들어가지 않는 / 그리고 전기초인종이 있었다 / 그리고 그 초인종으론 / 어떤 인간의 손도 울리게 할 수 없는

D. 1. Expenses had been greater / than she had calculated. 2. Rapidly she pulled down her hair / and let it fall / to its full length. 3. It surely had been made / for Jim / and no one else. 4. As soon as she saw it, / she knew / that it must be Jim's.

SCENE 6

"If Jim doesn't kill me," she said to herself, /
짐이 나를 죽이지 않는다면 그녀가 혼잣말을 했다 /

"before he takes a second look at me, /
그가 나를 한 번 더 쳐다보기 전에 /

he'll say I look / like a Coney Island chorus girl.
그는 내가 보인다고 할 거야 / 코니아일랜드의 합창단 소녀처럼

But what could I do / -oh! what could I do /
그러나 난 어떻게 하지 / -오! 내가 뭘 어떻게 할 수 있지 /

with a dollar and eighty-seven cents?"
1불 87센트로?

At 7 o'clock the coffee was made /
7시에 커피가 준비되었고 /

and the frying-pan was on the back of the stove /
그리고 프라이팬은 스토브에 올려져 있었고 /

hot and ready / to cook the chops.
달구어져서 준비가 되어있었다 / 고기토막을 요리할

Jim was never late.
짐은 늦게 오는 법이 없었다

Della doubled the watch chain / in her hand /
델라는 시곗줄을 접었다 / 손에서 /

and sat on the corner / of the table near the door /
그리고 테이블의 코너에 앉았다 / 문 근처에 있는 /

that he always entered.
(어떤 문?) 짐이 언제나 들어오는

Then she heard his step / on the stair away down /
그러자 그녀는 그의 발소리를 들었다 / 계단 아랫부분 멀리서 들리는 /

on the first flight, / and she turned white / for just a moment.
1층에 있는 층계의 그리고 그녀는 얼굴이 창백해졌다 / 잠시

She had a habit / for saying little silent prayers /
그녀는 버릇이 있었다 / 조용히 기도하는 /

about the simplest everyday things, /
아주 사소한 일상생활의 일에 대해서 /

and now she whispered: /
그리고 지금 그녀는 속삭였다 /

"Please God, make him think / I am still pretty."
신이시여, 그가 생각하게 해주세요 / 내가 여전히 예쁘다고

The door opened / and Jim stepped in / and closed it.
문이 열렸고 / 짐은 안으로 들어와서 / 문을 닫았다

He looked thin and very serious.
그는 말라보였고 매우 심각해 보였다

Poor fellow, / he was only twenty-two /
불쌍한 사람 / 그는 겨우 22살이었다 /

and to be burdened with a family!
그리고 한 가정을 책임져야하는 부담감을 갖고 있는

He needed a new overcoat / and he was without gloves.
그는 오버코트가 한 벌 필요했다 / 그리고 장갑도 없었다

Jim stopped inside the door, / as immovable / as a setter /
짐은 문 안쪽에서 멈추었다 / 움직이지 않고서 / 사냥개처럼 /

at the scent of quail.
메추라기의 냄새를 맡고

His eyes were fixed / upon Della, /
그의 시선은 고정되었다 / 델라에게 /

and there was an expression / in them /
그리고 어떤 표정이 있었다 / 그의 시선에는 /

that she could not read, / and it terrified her.
(어떤 표정일까?) 그녀가 읽을 수 없는 / 그리고 그 표정은 그녀를 무섭게 만들었다

It was not anger, nor surprise, nor disapproval, nor horror,
그것은 화도, 놀라움도, 불만도, 공포도,

nor any of the sentiments /
어떤 감정도 아니었다 /

that she had been prepared for.
(그런 감정에) 그녀가 마음의 준비를 했던

He simply stared at her / fixedly /
그는 그저 그녀를 응시했다 / 꼼짝하지 않고 /

with that peculiar expression on his face.
얼굴에 특이한 표정을 한 채로

setter 사냥개 scent 냄새 quail 메추라기 disapproval 불만 sentiment 감정 prepared for 마음의 준비를 한

SCENE 7

Della wriggled off the table / and went for him.
델라는 테이블에서 꿈틀거리며 일어서서 / 그에게 다가갔다

"Jim, darling," she cried, / "don't look at me / that way.
짐, 자기야 그녀가 외쳤다 / 날 쳐다보지 마요 / 그런 식으로

I had my hair cut off / and sold it /
나는 머리카락을 잘라서 / 팔았어요 /

because I couldn't have lived through Christmas /
왜냐하면 크리스마스를 보낼 수 없었기 때문이야 /

without giving you a present.
너에게 선물을 주지 않고

It'll grow out again -you won't mind, will you?
머리카락은 다시 자랄 거야 -괜찮지, 그렇지 않아요?

I just had to do it.
그래야만 했었어

My hair grows awfully fast.
나는 머리카락이 엄청 빨리 자라

Say 'Merry Christmas!' Jim, and let's be happy.
'메리 크리스마스' 라고 말해봐 짐 그리고 즐겁게 지내자고

You don't know / what a nice -what a beautiful, nice gift /
당신은 모를 거야 / 얼마나 근사하고 -얼마나 예쁘고 멋진 선물을 /

I've got for you."
내가 당신을 위해 사왔는지

"You've cut off your hair?" asked Jim, slowly, /
머리를 잘랐다고 짐이 천천히 물었다 /

as if he had not taken in / that patent fact /
마치 그가 이해하지 못한 듯이 / 명백한 사실을 /

yet even after the hardest mental labor.
심각한 정신적인 노동을 했음에도 불구하고

"Cut it off and sold it," said Della.
머리 잘라서 팔았어 델라가 말했다

"Don't you like me / just as well, anyhow?
너는 내가 좋지 / 여전히 어쨌든

I'm me / without my hair, / ain't I?"
여전히 나는 나니까 / 머리가 없어도 / 안 그래?

Jim looked about the room / curiously.
짐은 방을 둘러봤다 / 이상한 듯이

"You say your hair is gone?" he said, /
머리카락이 없어졌다고? 그는 말했다 /

with an air almost of idiocy.
거의 바보 같은 표정으로

"You needn't look for it," said Della.
(머리카락을) 찾을 필요 없어   델라가 말했다

"It's sold, I tell you - sold and gone, too.
팔았어   내가 말했듯이 – 팔아서 없어졌어

It's Christmas Eve, boy.
크리스마스이브예요, 여보

Be good to me, / for it went for you.
나에게 잘 해줘 /   왜냐하면 내 머리는 당신을 위해서 팔렸으니까

Maybe the hairs of my head were numbered," /
내 머리카락의 개수는 셀 수 있을 거야 /

she went on / with sudden serious sweetness, /
그녀는 말을 계속 했다 / 갑자기 매우 상냥하게 /

"but nobody could ever count my love / for you.
그러나 아무도 내 사랑은 셀 수가 없지요 /   당신에 대한

Shall I put the chops on, Jim?"
고기를 불에 올려놓을까요, 짐?

Key Expression

"have" 동사가 사역동사로 쓰일 때

have; 이 동사에 주어가 누군가에게 어떤 일을 "하게 하다, 시키다"라는 의미가 있다.
I had my hair cut off.
나는 (누군가에게) 시켰다 / 내 머리를 자르게
I had my students wait in the classroom.
나는 하게했다 / 학생들이 교실에서 기다리게 (했다)

---

wriggle 꿈틀거리며 움직이다 wriggle off 꿈틀거리며 일어서다 live through (어려운 시기를) 견디다, 이겨내다
take in (주로 부정문에서 보고 들은 것을) 이해하다 patent 명백한 mental 정신적인 as well 마찬가지로, 같이
curiously 이상한 듯이, 진기한 듯이 air 표정 idiocy 백치, 어리석음 number 수를 확인하다, 세다

SCENE 8

Out of his trance / Jim seemed quickly to wake.
얼떨떨한 상태에서 벗어나 /   짐은 재빨리 정신을 차린 것 같았다

He enfolded / his Della.
그는 포옹했다 /   델라를

For ten seconds / let us regard / with discreet scrutiny /
10초 동안 /   한번 생각해보자 /   신중하고 정밀하게 /

some inconsequential object / in the other direction.
별로 중요하지 않을 것을 /   다른 방향에서

Eight dollars a week or a million a year
1주일에 8불이든 1년에 1백만 불이든

-what is the difference?
- 뭐가 다를까?

A mathematician or a wit would give you the wrong answer.
수학자나 현자는 틀린 대답을 할지도 모른다

The magi brought valuable gifts, / but that was not among
동방박사는 귀중한 선물을 가져왔다 /   그러나 그 해답은 그 선물 속에도 없다

them. This dark assertion will be illuminated / later on.
이러한 불분명한 말의 뜻은 밝혀질 것이다 /   나중에

Jim drew a package / from his overcoat pocket /
짐은 꾸러미를 꺼냈다 /   오버코트 주머니에서 /

and threw it / upon the table.
그리고 던졌다 /   테이블 위에

"Don't make any mistake, Dell," he said,
 오해하지 마라, 델라   그가 말했다

"about me. I don't think / there's anything /
 나에 대해서   나는 생각하지 않아 /   대단한 것이 있다고 /

in the way of a haircut or a shave or a shampoo /
머리를 깎든 면도를 하든 머리를 감든 간에 /

that could make me like my girl / any less.
(그런 일이) 내가 너를 (더 적게) 좋아하게 만드는 /   조금이라도 더 조금

But if you'll unwrap / that package /
그러나 네가 풀어본다면 /   그 꾸러미를 /

you may see / what I felt / a while at first."
너는 알 게 될 거야 /   어떤 생각을 내가 했는지 / 잠시 동안 처음에

80   O. Henry's Short Stories

White fingers tore at / the string and paper.
하얀 손가락이 풀어헤쳤다 / 꾸러미의 끈과 포장지를

And then an ecstatic scream of joy; / and then, alas!
그 다음에 황홀한 기쁨의 탄성을 질렀다 / 그 다음에는 맙소사!라고 소리를 질렀다

a quick feminine change to / hysterical tears and wails, /
여성답게 빠르게 변하는 사건이 (발생했다) / 신경질적인 눈물과 통곡으로 /

necessitating / the immediate employment /
(그래서) 필요하게 했다 / 즉시 사용하는 것을 /

of all the comforting powers of the lord of the flat.
이 아파트 주인의 모든 위로하는 능력을

For there lay / The Combs - the set of combs,
왜냐하면 그곳에(테이블위에) 가지런히 놓여있었다 / 빗들이 - 빗 세트가 /

side and back, / that Della had seen /
옆머리와 뒷머리에 쓰는 / (그 빗 세트를) 델라가 본적이 있고 /

in a Broadway window / and loved for long.
오랫동안 브로드웨이 상점 진열장에서 / 오랫동안 갖기를 원했던

Beautiful combs, / pure tortoise shell, / with jewelled rims, /
아름다운 빗이었고 / 진짜 거북이 등껍질로 만든 / 보석을 박은 가장자리가 있고 /

perfect / for the beautiful hair.
꼭 어울리는 / 잘라버린 아름다운 머리카락에

They were expensive combs, / she knew, /
그것들은 비싼 빗이라는 것을 / 그녀가 알고 있었고 /

and her heart had simply craved and yearned over / them /
그리고 그녀의 가슴은 그저 갈망하고 동경했다 / 그것들을 /

without the least hope of possession.
가질 수 있다는 최소한의 희망도 없이

And now, they were hers, /
그리고 이제 그것들은 그녀의 것이 되었다 /

but the tresses / that should have adorned /
그러나 치렁치렁한 머리는 / (그것을) 갈망했었던 /

the coveted adornments / were gone.
동경하던 장식품을 / 없어졌다

---

trance 얼떨떨한 상태, 망연자실 regard (어떤 감정으로) 보다, 대하다 discreet 신중한 scrutiny 정밀한 조사 inconsequential 중요하지 않은 wit 현자, 현인 magi 동방박사 assertion 단언, 주장 illuminate 밝히다 anything 대단한 것(일) unwrap 포장을 풀다 tear at 잡아 뜯다, 풀어헤치다 ecstatic 황홀한 feminine 여성의 wail 통곡 necessitate ~을 필요로 하다 rim 가장자리 crave 갈망하다 yearn 동경하다 tresses 치렁치렁한 여자의 머리 adorn 꾸미다 covet 동경하다 adornment 장식품

SCENE 9

But she hugged them / to her bosom, /
그러나 그녀는 빗들을 품었다 / 가슴에

and at length she was able to look up / with dim eyes /
그리고 마침내 그녀는 고개를 들 수 있었다 / (눈물 때문에) 침침한 눈을 하고

and a smile and say: / "My hair grows so fast, Jim!"
그리고 미소 지으면서 말할 수 있었다 / 내 머리는 엄청 빨리 자라, 짐!

And then Della leaped up / like a little singed cat /
그리고 나서 델라는 뛰어올랐다 / 털이 타버린 새끼 고양이처럼 /

and cried, "Oh, oh!"
그리고 외쳤다 "오, 오!" 라고

Jim had not yet seen / his beautiful present.
짐은 아직 보지 않았다 / 멋진 자신의 선물을

She held it out to him / eagerly upon her open palm.
그녀는 선물을 그에게 내밀었다 / 간절하게 펼친 손바닥쪽으로

The precious metal seemed to flash / with a reflection /
값비싼 금속(금 시곗줄)은 번쩍이는 듯 했다 / 나타내는 것처럼 /

of her bright and ardent spirit.
(무엇을?) 그녀의 밝고 타오르는 듯한 기분을

"Isn't it dandy, Jim? I hunted / all over the town /
근사하지 않아, 짐? 나는 뒤졌어 / 온 시내를 /

to find it. You'll have to look at the time /
그것 찾느라고 시간을 봐야할 걸 /

a hundred times a day / now.
하루에 1백번은 / 이제부터는

Give me your watch. I want to see / how it looks on it."
네 시계 줘봐 나는 보고 싶어 / 잘 어울리는지

Instead of obeying, / Jim flopped down on the couch /
짐은 델라의 말을 따르는 대신 / 소파에 풀썩 주저앉았다 /

and put his hands under the back of his head / and smiled.
그리고 양손을 머리 뒤에 대고 / 웃었다

"Dell," said he, /
델라 그가 말했다 /

"let's put our Christmas presents away and keep them a
우리 크리스마스 선물을 당분간 치워 버리자

while.

They're too nice to use / just at present.
선물은 쓰기에 너무 좋아 / 현재로서는

I sold the watch / to get the money / to buy your combs.
나는 시계를 팔았어 / 돈을 마련하려고 / 빗을 살

And now / I suppose / we should have dinner."
그리고 지금 / 내가 생각하기엔 / 우리는 저녁을 먹어야해

Key Expression

1) 뭔가 "잘 어울리다" 라고 표현할 때

I want to see / how it(the watch chain) looks / on it(the watch)."
나는 보고 싶어 / 어떻게 시계 줄이 보이는지 / 시계에 연결하면
(잘 어울리는지)

The gold watch suits you well.
금시계는 너에게 잘 어울려

The shirt and the tie match.
셔츠와 넥타이는 잘 어울려

The shirt and the tie go well together.
셔츠와 넥타이는 잘 어울려

This cap becomes you.
이 모자는 너에게 잘 어울려

2) too 형용사 to 부정사

"too 형용사"는 "너무나(지나치게)"라는 뜻으로 "너무나, 지나치게(too)"라는 단어엔 부정적인 의미가 포함되어 있다. 그리고 "too" 다음에 오는 "to 부정사"는 "~하기에"라고 해석한다. "too(지나치게, 너무나)에 있는 부정적인 의미 때문에 "to 부정사(to +동사원형)"를 "~할 수 없다"라고 해석하기도 한다.

They're too nice to use just at present.
그들은 너무 좋아 / 사용하기엔 / 현재 (그래서 사용할 수 없다)

This soup is too salty to eat.
이 수프는 너무나 짜다 / 먹기에 (그래서 먹을 수 없다)

His offer is too good to be true.
그의 제안은 지나치게 좋다 / 사실로 믿어지기에 (그래서 믿어지지 않는다)

This box is too heavy to lift.
이 상자는 너무나 무겁다 / 들기에 (그래서 들 수 없다)

This watch is too expensive to buy.
이 시계는 너무나 비싸다 / 사기에 (그래서 살수 없다)

bosom 가슴 dim 침침한, 희미한 singed (털이) 탄, 그을린 flash 번쩍이다 reflection 반사 ardent 불타는
spirit 기분 dandy 멋진, 근사한 flop down 털썩 앉다

SCENE 10

The magi, / as you know, / were wise men /
동방박사들은 / 여러분도 아시다시피 / 현자였다 /

-wonderfully wise men /
엄청나게 현명한 사람들 /

- who brought gifts / to the Babe in the manger.
(그리고 그들은) 선물을 가져왔다 / 말구유 속에 있던 아기 예수에게

They invented the custom / of giving Christmas presents.
그들은 관습을 만들었다 / 크리스마스 선물을 주는

Being wise, / their gifts were no doubt wise ones, /
현명했기 때문에 / 동방박사의 선물 역시 의심할 바 없이 현명한 것이었다 /

possibly bearing the privilege /
(그리고) 아마도 특권도 있었을 것이다 /

of exchange in case of duplication.
중복된(같은 것일) 경우엔 바꿀 수 있는

And here I have lamely related to you /
그리고 여기서 나는 어설프게 당신에게 이야기했다 /

the uneventful narrative / of two foolish children /
평범한 이야기를 / 두 어리석은 어린이의 /

in a flat / who most unwisely sacrificed / for each other /
아파트에 살고 있는 / (그리고 두 사람은) 현명하지 못하게 희생시켰다 / 서로를 위해 /

the greatest treasures of their house.
집에서 가장 값진 보물을

But let me speak a last word / to the wise of these days /
그러나 마지막 말을 하겠다 / 오늘날의 현명한 사람들에게 /

of all who give gifts / these two were the wisest.
선물을 주는 모든 사람 중에서도 / 이 둘이 가장 현명한 사람들이었다

Of all who give and receive gifts, /
선물을 주고받는 모든 사람 중에서 /

such as they are wisest.
이 둘과 같은 사람들은 가장 현명하다

Everywhere they are wisest.
어디를 봐도 그들이 가장 현명하다

They are the magi.
이 둘이 동방박사다

Key Expression

동사와 관계명사의 쓰임새에 주의한다.

I have lamely related / to you /
나는 어설프게 이야기했다 / 당신에게 (어떤 말을 했나?)
*relate(이야기하다, 말하다)를 보면, "누구에게", "어떤 이야기(말)"를 할 것인지 예측한다.

the uneventful narrative / of two foolish children / in a flat /
평범한 이야기를 / (어떤 이야기일까?) 두 어리석은 어린이에 대한 / 아파트에 살고 있는 /
who most unwisely sacrificed / for each other / the greatest treasures of their house.
(그리고 두 사람은 어떤 사람일까?) 현명하지 못하게 희생시켰다 / 서로를 위해 / 집에서 가장 값진 보물을
*관계대명사로 쓰인 "who"를 보면, 앞에 나온 "two foolish children"(두 어리석은 어린이; 델라와 그녀의 남편)를 더 자세히 말하려 한다는 것을 예측한다.
*"sacrifice"라는 동사를 보면, "누구"를 위해 "무엇을" 희생하는지 예측한다.

Of all who; ~하는 사람 중에서

Of all who give gifts / these two were the wisest.
선물을 주는 모든 사람 중에서도 / 이 둘이 가장 현명한 사람들이었다.

---

magi 동방박사 babe in the manger 아기예수 privilege 특권 in case of ~할 경우에, ~인 경우에 duplication 중복, 복사 lamely 어설프게 relate 이야기하다 uneventful 아무 일도 없는, 무사 평온한 narrative 이야기 such as ~와 같은

85

Quiz 5

A. 내용 이해하기
다음 문장을 읽고 본문의 내용과 맞으면 T(True), 틀리면 F(False)를 쓰세요.

1. Jim was fascinated with Della's new hair style.
2. Della didn't like Jim's present.
3. Jim sold his gold watch chain in order to buy Della a gift.
4. Della and Jim couldn't have dinner because they had hurted each other.

B. 단어
다음 제시된 단어의 설명을 읽고, 어떤 단어의 정의를 설명하는지 아래의 박스에서 찾아 써 보세요.

1. to make something much clearer and easier to understand
2. careful about what you say or do
3. a feeling that you do not like an idea or somebody's behavior
4. a special advantage that is given to one person
5. fine or good
6. being in a state of extreme happiness and excitement
7. a statement saying or declaring that you strongly believe
8. to make something beautiful or attractive
9. The act or procedure of making an exact copy of an original
10. careful and thorough examination
11. to turn or twist your body backwards and forwards with small movements
12. a feeling you have of something
13. to burn the surface of something slightly

> disapproval sentiment wriggle discreet scrutiny assertion
> illuminate ecstatic adorn singe dandy privilege duplication

Answer
A. 1. F 2. F 3. F 4. F
B. 1. illuminate 2. discreet 3. disapproval 4. privilege 5. dandy 6. ecstatic 7. assertion 8. adorn
9. duplication 10. scrutiny 11. wriggle 12. sentiment 13. singe

C. 직독직해

아래에 제시된 문장을 직독직해로 해석해보세요.

1. His eyes were fixed / upon Della, / and there was an expression / in them / that she could not read, / and it terrified her.

   →

2. "You say your hair is gone?" he said, / with an air almost of idiocy.

   →

3. They were expensive combs, / she knew, / and her heart had simply craved and yearned over / them.

   →

4. The precious metal seemed to flash / with a reflection of her bright and ardent spirit.

   →

D. 동시통역

아래에 제시된 직독직해를 보고, 영어로 말해보세요.

1. "신이시여, 그가 생각하게 해주세요. / 내가 여전히 예쁘다고"

   →

2. "짐, 자기야" 그녀가 외쳤다. / "날 쳐다보지 마요 / 그런 식으로

   →

3. 당신은 모를 거야 / 얼마나 예쁘고 멋진 선물을 / 내가 사왔는지"

   →

4. 그녀는 선물을 그에게 내밀었다 / 간절하게 / 펼쳐진 손바닥 위에

   →

Answer

C. 1. 그의 시선은 고정되었다 / 델라에게 / 그리고 어떤 표정이 있었다 / 그의 시선에는 / (어떤 표정일까?) 그녀가 읽을 수 없는 / 그리고 그 표정은 그녀를 무섭게 만들었다. 2. "머리카락이 없어졌다고?" 그는 말했다 / 거의 바보 같은 표정으로 3. 그것들은 비싼 빗이라는 것을 / 그녀가 알고 있었고 / 그리고 그녀의 가슴은 그저 갈망하고 동경했다 / 그것들을 4. 값비싼 금속(금시계 줄)은 번쩍이는 듯 했다 / 나타내는 것처럼 / (무엇을?) 그녀의 밝고 타오르는 듯한 기분을

D. 1. "Please God, make him think / I am still pretty." 2. "Jim, darling," she cried, / "don't look at me / that way. 3. You don't know / what a beautiful, nice gift / I've got for you." 4. She held a present out to him / eagerly / upon her open palm.

Two Thanksgiving Day Gentlemen
추수감사절의 두 신사

SCENE 1

There is one day / that is ours.
하루가 있다 / (그날은) 우리의 날인

There is one day / when all we Americans /
어떤 날이 있다 / (그날에) 모든 미국인들이 /

who are not self-made / go back to the old home /
(어떤 미국인?) 자수성가하지 못한 / 자신들의 옛날 집으로 돌아간다 /

to eat a big dinner / and marvel /
만찬을 먹기 위해 / 그리고 이상하게 여긴다 /

how much nearer to the porch the old pump looks /
얼마나 가깝게 현관에서 낡은 펌프가 보이는지 /

than it used to. Bless the day.
예전보다 이 날을 축복하자

President Roosevelt gives it to us.
루즈벨트 대통령이 우리에게 이 날을 줬다

Sometimes he talks / about the Puritans /
가끔씩 그는 이야기를 한다 / 청교도들에 대해여 /

who had the first Thanksgiving.
(어떤 청교도들?) 첫 번째 추수감사제를 지냈던

But we don't just remember / who they were.
하지만 우리는 기억하지 못할 뿐이다 / 그들이 누군지는

They were some people / who landed on Plymouth Rocks.
그들은 사람들이었다 / (어떤 사람들?) 플리머스 바위에 상륙했던

Well, that sounds more familiar.
글쎄, 그건 좀 더 친숙하게 들리는데

Lots of us have had to come down to hens /
많은 미국인들이 암탉을 먹게 되었다 /

since the Turkey Trust was formed.
칠면조 조합이 결성된 때부터

The big city / east of the cranberry bogs / has made /
대도시는 /   크랜베리 습지의 동쪽에 있는 /   만들었다 /

Thanksgiving Day an institution.
추수감사절을 관습으로

The last Thursday in November is the only day in the year /
11월 마지막 목요일은 연중 단 하루뿐인 날이다 /

on which we have turkey / for Thanksgiving dinner.
(그날에) 미국인들이 칠면조를 먹는 /   추수감사절 만찬으로

It is the one day / that is purely American.
이 날은 유일한 날이다 /   (어떤 유일한 날?) 순수하게 미국적인

Yes, a day of celebration, exclusively American.
그렇다, 축하하는 날 /   완전히 미국적인 (날이다)

And now the story / is to prove to you /
그리고 이제 (말하려는) 이야기는 /   당신에게 입증할 것이다 /

that we have traditions / on this side of the ocean /
(무엇을 입증할까?) 우리는 전통을 갖고 있다고 / 대양의 이쪽에서

that are getting older / at a much more rapid rate /
(그 전통이란?) 정착되고 있는 /   더욱더 훨씬 빠른 속도로 /

than those of England are /
영국의 전통보다 /

-thanks to our git-up and enterprise.
우리의 패기와 모험심 덕분에

Stuffy Pete took his seat / on the third bench / to the right /
스터피 피트는 앉았다 /   세 번째 벤치에 /   오른쪽에서 /

as you enter Union Square / from the east, /
(어떤 오른쪽?) 여러분들이 유니온 스퀘어 공원을 들어갈 때 / 동쪽에서 /

at the walk opposite the fountain.
(동쪽이란?) 분수대 반대편 길이 있는

Every Thanksgiving Day / for nine years /
추수감사절 때마다 /   9년 동안 /

he had taken his seat there / promptly at 1 o'clock.
그는 거기에 앉았다 /   정확히 1시에

Every time, / things had happened to him /
그가 그럴 때마다 /   (좋은) 일이 그에게 생겼다 /

marvel 이상하게 여기다 Puritan 청교도 land 상륙하다 come down to 결국 ~이 되다 trust 조합 bog 습지
institution 관습 exclusively 완전히, 오로지 thanks to ~ 덕분에 git-up 패기, 일어서는 것 enterprise 기업
promptly 정확히

-Charles Dickensy things /
(그 좋은 일이란?) 찰스 디킨즈의 소설에서나 나올 법한 일이다 /

that swelled his waistcoat above his heart, /
그의 심장 위의 조끼를 불룩하게 만들고 /

and equally on the other side.
반대(심장아래)편도 똑같이 (그렇게 만드는)

Key Expression

문장부호 dash(-)를 사용하여 앞에 언급한 좋은 일(things)을 강조하고 설명한다.

Every Thanksgiving Day / for nine years /
추수감사절 때마다 / 9년 동안 /
he had taken his seat there / promptly at 1 o'clock.
그는 거기에 앉았다 / 정확히 1시에
Every time, / things had happened to him /
그가 그럴 때마다 / (좋은) 일이 그에게 생겼다 /
-Charles Dickensy things /
(그 좋은 일이란 무엇일까?) 찰스 디킨즈의 소설에서나 나올 법한 일이다 /
that swelled his waistcoat above his heart, /
(소설에 나오는 내용은?) 그의 심장 위의 조끼를 불룩하게 만들고(기쁨으로) /
and equally on the other side.
반대(심장아래)편도 똑같이 (잘 먹어서 불룩하게 만드는 일)

swell 부풀다

SCENE 2

But today Stuffy Pete's appearance /
그러나 오늘 스터피 피트가 나타난 것은 /

at the annual trysting place /
매년 만나는 약속 장소에 /

seemed to have been rather the result of habit /
버릇의 결과(버릇 때문에 생긴 일)인 것 같았다 /

than of the yearly hunger /
1년에 한번 느끼는 허기 때문이라기보다는 /

which, as the philanthropists seem to think, /
(일년에 한번 느끼는 허기란?) 박애주의자들이 생각하는 것 같다 /

afflicts the poor / only on Thanksgiving Day.
가난한 사람들을 괴롭힌다고 / 단지 추수감사절 날에만

Certainly Pete was not hungry.
분명히 피트는 배고프지 않았다

He had just come / from a feast /
그는 방금 돌아왔다 /   성찬을 먹고 /

that had left him of his powers /
(그 성찬은) 그에게서 힘을 뺏어버린 /

barely those of respiration and locomotion.
간신히 숨을 쉬고 움직일 수 있는 (힘을)

His eyes were like two pale gooseberries /
그의 눈은 두개의 창백한 구즈베리 같았다 /

firmly imbedded / in a swollen and gravy-smeared mask /
단단히 박혀있는 / 부풀고 고깃국을 바른 가면에 /

of putty. His breath came in short wheezes; /
(어떤 가면?) 퍼티 가루로 만든. 그의 숨소리는 짧게 색색거렸다 /

a senatorial roll of fat tissue / denied a fashionable set /
(왜?) 상원 의원처럼 두꺼운 지방 조직의 덩어리 때문에 / 유행의 흐름에 어울리지 않았다 /

to his upturned coat collar.
코트 깃을 세우는(유행)

---

annual 매년 tryst ~와 만날 약속을 하다 place 장소 philanthropist 박애주의자 afflict 괴롭히다 feast 향연, 잔치, 성찬 barely 간신히 respiration 호흡 locomotion 이동 firmly imbedded 단단히 박힌 smear (~에 끈적거리는 것을) 바르다 gravy-smeared 고깃국을 바른 putty 퍼티 가루(유리창을 창문에 고정시킬 때 사용하는 하얀 물질로 건조되면 부드러운 백색 물질로 변함) wheeze 색색거리는 숨소리 deny 부정하다, 멀리하다

Buttons that had been sewed upon his clothes /
단추는 (어떤 단추?) 그의 옷에 꿰맨 /

by kind Salvation fingers / a week before /
친절한 구세군의 손으로 /　　　　　　1주일 전에 /

flew like popcorn; / strewing the earth / around him.
옥수수 알맹이처럼 튕겨나갔다 / (그리고) 땅에 흩어졌다 /　그의 주위에

Ragged he was, / with a split shirt front /
그의 모습은 초라했다 /　　찢어진 셔츠 앞쪽이 /

open to the wishbone; / but the November breeze, /
가슴골까지 드러났기에 /　　　그러나 11월의 산들바람은 /

carrying fine snowflakes, / brought him /
가는 눈송이를 실은 /　　　　　그에게 데리고 왔다 /

only a grateful coolness.
고맙게 느끼는 시원함을(산들바람 때문에 그는 고맙게 느낄 정도로 시원했다)

For Stuffy Pete was overheated / with the caloric produced /
왜냐하면 스터피 피트는 열이 많이 났다 /　　생긴 열량 때문에 /

by a bountiful dinner, /
진수성찬의 저녁식사를 해서 /

beginning with oysters /
(진수성찬은) 굴부터 시작해서 /

and ending with plum pudding, /
건포도 푸딩으로 끝나고 /

and including (it seemed to him) /
그리고 포함하고 있었다 (그에게는 그렇게 보였다) /

all the roast turkey and baked potatoes and chicken salad
모든 구운 칠면조와 구운 감자와 치킨 샐러드

and fruit pie and ice cream / in the world.
그리고 과즙 파이와 아이스크림을 /　　이세상의

So he sat, gorged, / and gazed upon the world /
그래서 그는 배불리 먹고 앉아서 / 세상을 응시했다 /

with after-dinner contempt.
저녁 식사를 한 후 경멸스럽게

The meal had been an unexpected one.
식사는 예상하지 않았던 것이었다.

He was passing a red brick mansion /
그는 빨간 벽돌로 된 대저택을 지나가고 있었다 /

near the beginning of Fifth avenue, / in which lived /
5번가의 어귀 근처에 있는 /　　　　　　(그 집에는) 살고 있었다 /

two old ladies of ancient family and a reverence for
오래된 가문이며 전통을 존중하는 두 분의 할머니가

traditions. They even denied / the existence of New York, /
그 할머니들은 부정했다 / 뉴욕의 존재를 /

and believed / that Thanksgiving Day was declared solely
그리고 믿고 있었다 / 추수감사절은 오로지 워싱턴 스퀘어를 위해서 선포된 것으로

for Washington Square.

ragged 초라한 grateful 고맙게 여기는 overheat 열이 많이 났다 bountiful 풍성한, 풍부한 oyster 굴 plum pudding 건포도 푸딩 gorge 배불리 먹다, 게걸스럽게 먹다 gaze 응시하다 contempt 경멸 mansion 대저택 avenue …가(街), 대로 reverence 존경 declare 선언하다 solely 단독으로

SCENE 3

One of their traditional habits was to station /
전통적인 습관 중 하나는 세워두는(배치하는) 것이었다 /

a servant at the back gate / with orders /
하인을 뒷문에 / (어떤 하인일까?) 명령을 받은 /

to admit the first hungry traveler /
(어떤 명령?) 첫 번째 굶주린 나그네를 (저택 안으로) 들여놓으라는 /

that walked by / after the hour of noon had struck, /
(어떤 나그네?) 지나가는 / 정오 시간이 된 후 /

and banquet him / until he could eat his fill.
그리고 그 나그네를 진수성찬으로 대접하라고 / 배불리 먹을 때까지

Stuffy Pete happened to pass / by on his way to the park, /
스터피 피트는 우연히 지나가게 되었다 / 공원으로 가는 길에 /

and the servants gathered him in /
그리고 하인들이 그를 거두어들였고, /

and upheld the custom of the castle.
이 집의 전통을 유지했다.

After Stuffy Pete had gazed / straight before him for ten
스터피 피트가 응시한 후에 / 10분 동안 자신의 앞을 /

minutes / he felt a desire / to look in another direction.
그는 생각이 들었다 / 다른 곳을 쳐다보고 싶은.

With a tremendous effort / he moved /
엄청 애를 쓰며 / 그는 움직였다 /

his head slowly to the left.
고개를 천천히 왼쪽으로

And then his eyes bulged out / fearfully, /
그러자 그의 눈은 튀어나왔다 / 겁에 질려서 /

and his breath ceased, / and his feet in their torn shoes /
그리고 숨이 멈추었다 / 그리고 찢어진 신발 속에 그의 발은 /

at the ends of his short legs / wriggled and rustled /
짧은 다리 끝에 있던 / (발이) 꿈틀거렸고 활발히 움직였다 /

on the gravel. For the Old Gentleman was coming /
자갈 위에서 왜냐하면 늙은 신사가 오고 있었기 때문이었다 /

across Fourth avenue toward his bench.
4번가를 지나서 그의 벤치 쪽으로

Every Thanksgiving Day / for nine years /
추수감사절마다 / 9년 동안 /

the Old Gentleman had come there / and found /
이 늙은 신사는 거기로 왔다 / 그리고 발견했다 /

Stuffy Pete on his bench. That was a thing /
벤치에 앉아 있는 스터피 피트를 이런 일은 것이었다 /

that the Old Gentleman was trying to make a tradition of.
늙은 신사가 전통으로 만들려고 했던

Every Thanksgiving Day / for nine years /
추수감사절마다 / 9년 동안 /

he had found Stuffy there, / and had led him /
그는 스터피를 그곳에서 발견했다 / 그리고는 그를 데려갔고 /

to a restaurant / and watched / him eat a big dinner.
식당으로 / 지켜봤다 / 그가 푸짐하게 저녁 식사를 먹는 것을

They do those things / in England unconsciously.
사람들은 이런 일을 한다 / 영국에서는 무의식적으로

But this is a young country, / and nine years is not so bad.
그러나 여기는 신생 국가다 / 그리고 9년은 그렇게 적은 세월이 아니다

The Old Gentleman was a staunch American patriot, /
늙은 신사는 충실한 미국의 애국자였다 /

and considered / himself a pioneer in American tradition.
그리고 생각했다 / 자기 자신이 미국 전통을 만드는 선구자라고

In order to become picturesque /
아름답게 하려면 /

we must keep on doing one thing / for a long time /
우리는 한 가지 일을 지속적으로 해야 한다 / 오랫동안 /

without ever letting it get away from us.
한번도 빼먹지 않고

Something like collecting the weekly dimes /
매주 10센트씩(보험료를) 거둬가는 일처럼 /

in industrial insurance. Or cleaning the streets.
기업보험회사에서 또는 거리를 청소하는 것처럼

---

station 배치하다, 세워두다 admit 들이다 strike (strike-struck-struck) (때가) 오다, (시계가) 때를 알리다
banquet 대접하다 eat one's fill 배불리 먹다 gather in 거두어들이다 uphold (관습, 전통을) 유지하다
tremendous (크기, 정도가) 엄청난 bulge 튀어나오다, 부풀다 fearfully 겁에 질려서 cease 멈추다
wriggle 꿈틀거리다 rustle 활발하게 움직이다 unconsciously 무의식적으로 staunch 충실한, 지지가 있는
patriot 애국자 pioneer 선구자 picturesque 아름다운, 그림 같은

SCENE 4

The Old Gentleman moved, / straight and stately, /
그 늙은 신사가 움직였다 /   곧바로 품위 있게 /

toward the Institution / that he was rearing.
관습을 향해서 /   (어떤 관습?) 그가 키우고 있던

Truly, feeding Stuffy Pete once a year / was nothing /
사실은 일년에 한번씩 스터피 피트를 먹이는 것은 /   아니었다 /

national in its character, /
전국적인 성격을 띤 것이 /

such as the Magna Charta or jam for breakfast /
마그나 카르타 대헌장이나 아침에 잼을 먹는 것처럼 /

was in England. But it was a step. It was almost feudal.
영국에서   그러나 그것은 첫걸음이었다. (이제는) 그것은 거의 봉건제도처럼 굳어 있었다

It showed, at least, / that a Custom was not impossible to
그것은 최소한 보여줬다 /   (무엇을?) 관습을 만드는 것이 가능하다는 것을

New Y-ahem!-America.
뉴욕 아니 미국에서

The Old Gentleman was thin and tall and sixty.
그 늙은 신사는 마르고 키가 큰 60대였다

He was dressed all in black, / and wore the old-fashioned
그는 모두 검은 색으로 입었고 /   구닥다리의 안경을 쓰고 있었다 /

kind of glasses / that won't stay on your nose.
  (그런데 그 안경은) 코에 가만히 붙어 있지 않는

His hair was whiter and thinner than / it had been last year, /
그의 머리카락은 더 하얗게 되고 가늘어졌다 /   작년보다 /

and he seemed to make more use of his big, knobby cane /
그리고 그는 크고 우툴두툴한 지팡이를 더 많이 사용하는 것 같았다 /

with the crooked handle.
구부러진 손잡이가 있는

As his established benefactor came up /
관습처럼 정착된 후원자가 다가오고 있을 때 /

Stuffy wheezed and shuddered /
스터피는 숨을 색색거리고 몸을 떨었다 /

like some woman's over-fat pug /
안주인을 따라가던 너무 살찐 퍼그 개처럼 /

when a street dog bristles up at him.
거리에서 만난 개가 털을 곤두세울 때

He would have flown, / but he could not move /
(가능하다면) 그는 날아서 도망갔었을 것이다 / 그러나 그는 움직일 수 없었다 /

from his bench.
벤치에서

Well had the servants of the two old ladies done their work.
두 할머니의 하인들은 맡은 바 임부를 잘 해냈다

"Good morning," said the Old Gentleman.
안녕하세요   늙은 신사가 말했다

"I am glad to perceive /
나는 알게 되어서 기쁘군요 / (무엇을 알아서 기쁠까?)

that the vicissitudes of another year have spared /
또 한해의 변화는 해를 입히지 않은 것을 (알아서) /

you to move in health / about the beautiful world.
당신이 건강하게 움직일 수 있도록 /   아름다운 세상에서

Thanks to that blessing, / you and I could meet /
그런 축복덕분에 /   당신과 나는 만날 수 있지요 /

on this day of thanksgiving. If you will come with me, /
오늘 같은 추수 감사절에   만일 나와 함께 간다면 /

my man, / I will provide you / with a dinner /
형제여 /   대접하겠소 /   저녁식사를 /

that should make your physical being accord with the mental."
(어떤 저녁식사?) 당신의 육체와 정신을 조화롭게 하는

Key Expression

가정법과 직설법이 함께 쓰인 경우

"He would have flown"라는 표현을 사용하여 가정법으로 시작했지만, 그다음 문장인 "but he could not move from his bench."는 직설법을 사용했다. 오 헨리의 작품을 보면, 가끔씩 전통 문법의 틀에서 벗어난 표현이 나오지만, 이해할 수 없을 정도로 문법에서 벗어난 것은 아니다. 그래서 자신이 알고 있던 문법과 맞는지 아닌지 따지기보다는 의미를 이해할 필요가 있다. 마찬가지로 회화를 할때도 의미의 전달에 중점을 둘 필요가 있다.

He would have flown, (If he had been a bird) /
그는 날아서 도망갔었을 것이다 / (그가 새였다면; 가정법) /
but he could not move / from his bench.
그러나 그는 움직일 수 없었다 / 벤치에서 (직설법)

stately 당당하게, 품위 있게 rear 육성하다, 키우다 feudal 봉건의 knobby 우툴두툴한 establish 고정시키다, 확립하다 benefactor 후원자 shudder 몸을 떨다 bristle 털을 곤두세우다 perceive 지각하다, 이해하다 vicissitudes 변화, (인생의) 변천, 영고성쇠 spare 해를 입히지 않고 두다 accord ~와조화하다, 일치하다

Quiz 6

A. 내용 이해하기
다음 문장을 읽고 본문의 내용과 맞으면 T(True), 틀리면 F(False)를 쓰세요.

1. It was the Puritans that had the first Thanksgiving.
2. Stuffy was excited because he could go to a restaurant with the old gentleman.
3. The old gentleman had come to see Stuffy once a year for a decade.
4. Stuffy was glad to see the old gentleman again.

B. 단어
다음 제시된 단어의 설명을 읽고, 어떤 단어의 정의를 설명하는지 아래의 박스에서 찾아 써 보세요.

1. to feel great surprise at something
2. to look after young children or animals until they are fully grown
3. a feeling of great respect and love for something
4. the continuous changes that affect someone's life
5. to breathe with difficulty, making a hoarse whistling noise
6. the act of breathing
7. a company or a business organization
8. to stick out or swell up
9. to become larger in size or volume
10. to eat a lot until you are extremely full
11. to affect somebody in an unpleasant way, and make him suffer
12. a very good large meal
13. the ability to move from place to place

> marvel enterprise swell afflict feast respiration locomotion
> wheeze gorge reverence bulge rear vicissitudes

Answer
A. 1. T 2. F 3. F 4. F
B. 1. marvel 2. rear 3. reverence 4. vicissitudes 5. wheeze 6. respiration 7. enterprise 8. bulge 9. swell 10. gorge 11. afflict 12. feast 13. locomotion

C. 직독직해

아래에 제시된 문장을 직독직해로 해석해보세요.

1. There is one day / when all we Americans / who are not self-made / go back to the old home / to eat a big dinner.

   →

2. He had just come / from a feast / that had left him of his powers barely those of respiration and locomotion.

   →

3. One of their traditional habits was to station / a servant at the back gate / with orders / to admit the first hungry traveler / that walked by / after the hour of noon had struck, / and banquet him / until he could eat his fill.

4. Truly, feeding Stuffy Pete once a year / was nothing / national in its character, / such as the Magna Charta or jam for breakfast / was in England.

   →

D. 동시통역

아래에 제시된 직독직해를 보고, 영어로 말해보세요.

1. 이 날은 유일한 날이다 / (어떤 유일한 날?) 순수하게 미국적인

   →

2. 그는 빨간 벽돌로 된 대저택을 지나가고 있었다 / 5번가의 어귀 근처에 있는

   →

3. 엄청 애를 쓰며 / 그는 움직였다 / 고개를 천천히 / 왼쪽으로

   →

4. 그것은 일이었다 / 늙은 신사가 전통으로 만들려는

   →

Answer

C. 1. 어떤 날이 있다 / (그날에) 모든 미국인들이 / (어떤 미국인?) 자수성가하지 못한 / 자신들의 옛날 집으로 돌아간다 / 만찬을 먹기 위해
2. 그는 방금 돌아왔다 / 성찬을 먹고 / (그 성찬은) 그에게서 힘을 뺏어버렸다 / 간신히 숨을 쉬고 움직일 수 있는 (힘을) 3. 전통적인 습관 하나는 세워두는(배치하는) 것이었다 / 하인을 뒷문에 / (어떤 하인일까?) 명령을 받은 / (어떤 명령?) 첫 번째 굶주린 나그네를 (저택 안으로) 들여놓으라는 / (어떤 나그네?) 지나가는 / 정오 시간이 된 후 / 그리고 그 나그네를 진수성찬으로 대접하라는 (명령을 받은) / 배불리 먹을 때까지
4. 사실은 일년에 한번씩 스터피 피트를 먹이는 것은 / 아니었다 / 전국적인 성격을 띤 것이 / 마그나 카르타 대헌장이나 아침에 잼을 먹는 것처럼 / 영국에서

D. 1. It is the one day / that is purely American. 2. He was passing a red brick mansion / near the beginning of Fifth avenue. 3. With a tremendous effort / he moved / his head slowly to the left. 4. That was a thing / that the Old Gentleman was trying to make a tradition of.

SCENE 5

That is what the old Gentleman said / every time.
이것이 늙은 신사가 말하는 것이었다 / 매번

Every Thanksgiving Day for nine years.
추수감사절마다 9년 동안

The words themselves almost formed / an Institution.
이 말 자체가 거의 되었다 / 관습이

Nothing could be compared with them /
이것(전에 했던 말)과 비교할 만한 것은 없었다(최고였다) /

except the Declaration of Independence.
미국독립선언을 제외하고

Always before, / they had been music / in Stuffy's ears.
예전에는 항상 / 이러한 말들이 음악처럼 들렸었다 / 스터피의 귀에는

But now he looked up / at the Old Gentleman's face /
그러나 지금은 그는 바라보았다 / 늙은 신사의 얼굴을 /

with tearful agony in his own.
얼굴엔 눈물겹도록 괴로운 표정으로

The fine snow turned quickly to water / when it fell /
가느다란 눈송이가 거의 순식간에 녹았다 / 눈이 떨어지면 /

upon his perspiring brow. But the Old Gentleman shivered
땀이 나는 그의 이마에 그러나 늙은 신사는 약간 몸을 떨었고

a little / and turned his back to the wind.
바람을 등지고 있었다

Stuffy had always wondered / why the Old Gentleman
스터피는 항상 궁금했다 / 왜 늙은 신사가 슬퍼보였는지 /

looked sad / as he spoke. He did not know that /
그가 말할 때 그는 몰랐다 / (무엇을 몰랐는가?)

it was because he was wishing / every time /
그(슬퍼 보이는) 이유가 그는 바라고 있었기 때문이었다는 것을 / 매번

that he had a son / to succeed him.
(무엇을 바랬는가?) 아들이 있기를 / 그의 대를 이을

A son / who would come there / after he was gone /
(구체적으로) 아들을 (바랬다) / 여기에 올 / 그가 죽은 뒤에 /

-a son / who would stand proud and strong /
아들을 (바랬다) / 자랑스러워하고 그리고 당당하게 행동하는 /

before some subsequent Stuffy, / and say:
스터피의 뒤를 잇는 인물 앞에서 / 그리고 말할 수 있는 (아들을)

"In memory of my father." Then it would be an Institution.
"아버지를 기념하며" 라고 그러면 이러한 행동은 관습이 될 것이다

But the Old Gentleman had no relatives.
그러나 늙은 신사는 친척이 없었다

He lived in rented rooms /
그는 셋방에서 살고 있었다 /

in one of the decayed old family brownstone mansions /
낡고 쓰러져가는 갈색 돌로 지은 저택의 /

in one of the quiet streets east of the park.
공원 동쪽 조용한 거리에 있는

In the winter he raised a few flowers /
겨울에 그는 몇 종의 꽃을 키웠다 /

in a little conservatory / the size of a trunk.
작은 온실에서 / 여행용 트렁크 크기의

In the spring he walked / in the Easter parade.
봄에는 걸었다 / 부활절 퍼레이드에 참여해서

In the summer he lived / at a farmhouse /
여름에는 그는 살았다 / 농가에 /

in the New Jersey hills, / and sat / in a wicker armchair, /
뉴저지 언덕에 있는 / 그리고 앉아 있었다 / 버들가지로 만든 흔들의자에 /

speaking of a strange butterfly, /
(그때) 이야기했다 / 진귀한 나비에 대해서 /

that he hoped to find some day.
(그 나비를) 그는 언젠가 찾고 싶어 했던

In the autumn he fed Stuffy a dinner.
가을에는 그는 스터피에게 저녁을 먹였다

These were the Old Gentleman's occupations.
이것들이 늙은 신사가 하는 일이었다

> ### Key Expression
>
> **Nothing could be compared with 명사 or 명사구**
>
> "~와 비교할 만한 것이 없다, 최고다."라고 말하고 싶다면, "Nothing could be compared with" 다음에, 무엇인지에 해당되는 말만 첨가하면 된다.

agony 심한 고통 fine 가느다란, 미세한 perspire 땀을 흘리다 brow 이마 shiver (몸을) 떨다
succeed 계승하다 subsequent 다음의 decay 부패하다, 쇠퇴하다 conservatory 온실 Easter 부활절
wicker 버들가지 occupation 일, 활동

SCENE 6

Stuffy Pete looked up at the Old Gentleman /
스터피 피트는 늙은 신사를 바라보았다 /

for a half minute, / stewing and helpless /
30초 동안 / 애가타고 어쩔 줄 모르면서 /

in his own self-pity. The Old Gentleman's eyes were
자기연민으로 늙은 신사의 눈은 밝게 빛났다 /

bright / with the giving-pleasure.
  베푸는 즐거움 때문에

His face was getting more lined each year, /
그의 얼굴은 매년 주름이 많아지고 있었다 /

but his little black necktie was in as jaunty a bow /
그러나 그의 작은 검은 넥타이는 멋진 나비매듭으로 매여 있었다 /

as ever, / and his clothes were beautiful and white, /
언제나 / 그리고 그의 옷은 멋지고 흰색이었다 /

and his gray mustache was curled / at the ends.
그리고 그의 회색 수염은 곱슬곱슬했다 / 끝부분에

And then Stuffy made a noise / that sounded /
그 다음에 스터피가 소리를 냈다 / (그 소리는) 들리는 /

like peas bubbling in a pot. He intended to speak; /
냄비에서 콩이 끓는 것처럼 어떤 말을 하려고 했다 /

and as the Old Gentleman had heard /
그리고 늙은 신사가 들었으므로 /

the sounds nine times before, / he rightly construed /
(스피트의) 소리를 예전에 9번이나 / 그는 바로 해석했다 /

them into Stuffy's old way of acceptance.
그 소리를 (식사대접을) 스터피가 수락하는 일상적인 (표현) 방법으로

"Thank you, sir. I'll go with you, and much obliged.
감사합니다. 선생님. 함께 가지요 그리고 대단히 감사합니다.

I'm very hungry, sir." The coma of repletion /
저는 무지 배고파요, 선생님 포식으로 인해 정신이 혼미한 상태는 /

had not prevented / from entering Stuffy's mind /
방해하지 못했다 / 스터피의 마음으로 들어가는 것을 /

the conviction / that he was the basis of an Institution.
확신이 / 자신이 새로운 관습(전통)의 기반이라는 (확신이)
  (포식으로 혼미했지만 자신이 새로운 관습의 기반이라고
  확신할 수 밖에 없었다.)

His Thanksgiving appetite was not his own; /
그의 추수감사절의 식욕은 자기 것이 아니었다 /

it belonged to this kind old gentleman /
그것(식욕)은 이 친절한 노신사에게 속했다 /

by all the sacred rights of established custom, /
확립된 관습의 성스러운 권리에 따라 /

since the Old Gentleman had preempted it. /
왜냐하면 그 노신사가 권리를 미리 획득했기 때문이었다

True, America is free; / but in order to establish tradition /
정말, 미국은 자유의 나라다 /   그러나 전통을 수립하기 위해서는 /

some one must follow it / every year.
누군가 그 전통을 따라야한다 /   매년

The heroes are not all heroes of steel and gold.
영웅들은 반드시 강철과 금으로 된 것이 아니다

See one here / that wielded only weapons /
여기에 있는 한 영웅을 보라 / (그 영웅은) 무기만을 휘둘렀던 /

of iron, badly silvered, and tin.
(어떤 무기?) 엉성하게 은으로 도금한 쇠와 양철로 만든

The Old Gentleman led / his annual protege southward /
늙은 신사는 데리고 갔다 /   매년 보호하는 사람을 남쪽으로 /

to the restaurant, / and to the table /
식당을 향해 /   그리고 테이블로 (갔다) /

where the feast had always occurred.
그곳에서 항상 잔치가 열렸다

They were known / at this place.
그들은 알려졌다 /   이 식당에서

Key Expression

not ~ all(부분 부정); ~가 아니다, ~라고 할 수 없다.

He did not answer all the questions. 그가 대답한 것은 아니었다 / 모든 질문에
Not everyone likes the movie. 반드시 모든 사람이 좋아하는 것은 아니다 / 그 영화를
Not all people are kind. 반드시 모든 사람들이 친절한 것은 아니다.

stew 애가 타다, 마음을 졸이다 self-pity 자기연민 jaunty 멋진, 말쑥한 in a bow 나비매듭으로
bubble 부글부글 끓다 intend 의도하다 construe 해석하다 oblige (보통 수동형으로) 고맙게 여기다
much obliged; Thank you very much coma 혼수상태 repletion 포식 sacred 성스러운 established 확립된
preempt 미리 획득하다 protege 보호 받는 사람

SCENE 7

"Here comes the old guy," said a waiter, /

"the man buy the same bum a meal / every Thanksgiving."

The Old Gentleman sat across the table /

glowing like a pearl / at his corner-stone of future ancient

Tradition. The waiters heaped the table / with holiday food /

-and Stuffy, with a sigh / that was mistaken for hunger's

expression, / raised knife and fork / and carved the meat /

into thin slices. No hero ever fought /

valiantly against an enemy. Turkey, chops, soups, vegetables,

pies, disappeared before him / as fast as they could be served.

Gorged nearly to the uttermost / when he entered the

restaurant, / the smell of food had almost caused /

him to lose his honor as a gentleman, / but he rallied /

like a true knight. He saw the look / of beneficent happiness /

on the Old Gentleman's face / -a happier look /

than even a flower or a strange butterfly had ever brought

to it / -and he had not the heart to see / it wane.

In an hour Stuffy leaned back / with a battle won.
한 시간 후에 스터피는 (의자에) 기대었다 / 전투에서 이기고

"Thank you, sir," he puffed / like a leaky steam pipe; /
감사합니다, 선생님 그는 숨을 헐떡였다 / 구멍 난 증기 파이프처럼 /

"thank you / for a hearty meal."
감사합니다 / 풍성한 식사를 대접해주셔서

Then he arose heavily / with glazed eyes /
그 다음에 그는 힘겹게 일어났고 / 흐릿한 눈을 하고 /

and started toward the kitchen.
그리고 주방 쪽으로 가기 시작했다

A waiter turned him / about like a top, /
웨이터가 그를 돌렸고 / 팽이처럼 /

and pointed him toward the door.
그리고 그에게 문을 가리켰다

The Old Gentleman carefully counted out /
늙은 신사는 조심스럽게 셌다 /

$1.30 in silver change, / leaving / three nickels for the
1불 30센트를 은화 동전으로 / (그리고) 남겼다 / 세 개의 5센트 동전을 팁으로

waiter. They parted / as they did each year at the door, /
그들은 헤어졌다 / 매년 그랬듯이 문에서 /

the Old Gentleman going south, Stuffy north.
늙은 신사는 남쪽으로 갔고 스터피는 북쪽으로 갔다

Key Expression 🔑

스터피가 음식을 먹는 모습을 기사가 전투하는 장면에 비유

*식탁에 쌓인 음식을 먹는 모습은 적진에 뛰어들어 용감하게 싸우는 모습과 비슷하다.
No hero ever fought / valiantly against an enemy.
어떤 영웅도 지금까지 싸운 적이 없었다 / 용감하게 적과

*왕성한 식욕으로 음식을 먹는 모습은 기사가 온힘을 다해 싸우는 모습과 비슷하다.
He rallied / like a true knight.
그는 다시 (식욕을) 회복했다 / 진짜 기사처럼

*음식을 먹고 휴식하는 모습은 전투에 이기고 쉬는 모습과 비슷하다.
In an hour Stuffy leaned back with a battle won.
한 시간 후에 (의자에) 기대었다 / 스터피는 전투에서 이기고

---

bum 노숙자, 부랑자 corner-stone 초석 heap 수북하게 쌓다, 올려놓다 mistaken ~으로 오인된, 잘못 여겨진
carve (고기를) 썰다 valiantly 용감하게 gorge 배불리 먹다 to the uttermost 최대한도까지 honor 명예
rally (기력, 체력을) 회복하다 beneficent 인자한 wane 작아지다, 약해지다 puff 숨을 헐떡이다
hearty 충분한, 풍부한 glazed (눈, 표정이) 흐리멍텅한 part 헤어지다, 이별하다

SCENE 8

Around the first corner Stuffy turned, /
첫 번째 모퉁이를 스터피가 돌고나서 /

and stood for one minute.
그는 잠시 섰다

Then he fell to the sidewalk / like a sunstricken horse.
그 다음에 그는 인도에 쓰러졌다 / 더위 먹은 말처럼

When the ambulance came /
앰뷸런스가 왔을 때 /

the young surgeon and the driver cursed softly /
젊은 외과의사와 운전사는 좀 투덜거렸다 /

at his weight. There was no smell of whiskey /
스터피의 몸무게 때문에. 술 냄새가 나지 않았다 /

to justify a transfer / to the patrol wagon, /
인계하는 것을 정당화시킬 수 있을 정도로 / 경찰의 범인 호송차로 /

so Stuffy and his two dinners went to the hospital.
그래서 스터피와 2번 먹은 저녁식사는 병원으로 갔다

There they stretched him / on a bed / and began to test him /
병원에서 스터피의 몸을 펴놓았다 / 침대위에 / 그리고 그를 시험하기 시작했다 /

for strange diseases, / with the hope of getting a chance /
이상한 병이 있는지 / 실마리라도 얻지 않을까 하는 희망을 갖고 /

at some problem / with the scalpel.
어떤 문제를 해결할 수 있는 / 메스를 들고

And lo! an hour later another ambulance brought /
그런데 보라! 1시간 후에 또 다른 앰뷸런스가 데려왔다 /

the Old Gentleman. And they laid him on another bed /
그 늙은 신사를 그리고 병원사람들이 그를 다른 침대에 눕혔고 /

and spoke of appendicitis, /
맹장염이라고 이야기했다 /

for he looked good / for the bill.
왜냐하면 그는 신뢰할 수 있는 것처럼 보였기 때문에 / 치료비를 낼 수 있을 정도로

But pretty soon one of the young doctors met /
그러나 곧 젊은 의사 한명이 만났다 /

one of the young nurses / whose eyes / he liked, /
젊은 간호원을 / 그녀의 눈을 / 자기가 좋아했던

and stopped to chat with her / about the cases.
그리고 그녀와 이야기를 하기 위해 걸음을 멈췄다 / 두 환자에 대해서

"That nice old gentleman over there, now," he said, /
저 근사한 늙은 신사 말이야   의사가 말했다 /

"you wouldn't think / that was a case of almost
아마 생각하지 못할 걸 /   그 사람이 거의 굶어 죽을 뻔했던 환자였다는 것을

starvation. Proud old family, I guess.
             자존심 강한 오래된 집안이라고 나는 생각해

He told me / he hadn't eaten a thing / for three days."
그는 나한테 말했지 / 그는 아무것도 먹지 못했다고 /   사흘 동안

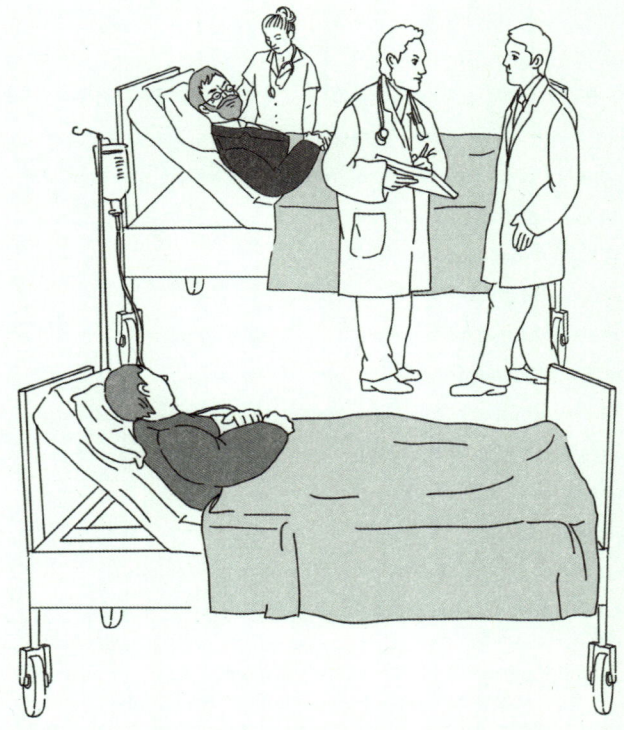

sunstricken 더위를 먹은 curse 욕을 퍼붓다, 악담을 하다 justify 정당화하다 transfer 인계, 이전
wagon 범인 호송차 scalpel 메스 appendicitis 맹장염 good 신뢰할 수 있는, 어울리는, 적절한 bill 비용, 치료비
case 환자 starvation 기아

Quiz 7

A. 내용 이해하기
다음 문장을 읽고 본문의 내용과 맞으면 T(True), 틀리면 F(False)를 쓰세요.

1. The old gentleman didn't have any kid to support his own institution.
2. Stuffy declined the old gentleman's invitation to the Thanksgiving day feast because he had enough.
3. Stuffy was hungry enough to eat up all of the meal the old gentleman bought for him.
4. The old gentleman was brought to a hospital due to appendicitis.

B. 단어
다음 제시된 단어의 설명을 읽고, 어떤 단어의 정의를 설명하는지 아래의 박스에서 찾아 써 보세요.

1. very important and greatly respected
2. to understand the meaning of a remark or action in a particular way
3. intense physical or mental pain
4. to breathe quickly and forcefully
5. to decrease in intensity or degree
6. a state of having been unconscious for a long time
7. to flow with a gurgling sound when water boils
8. showing kindness or helping people
9. to say bad things about someone because they have made you angry
10. to become stronger; recover
11. to sweat
12. to prove or show something to be right or reasonable
13. excessive fullness due to overeating

---
agony perspire bubble construe coma repletion sacred
rally beneficent wane puff curse justify

Answer

A. 1. T 2. F 3. F 4. F

B. 1. sacred 2. construe 3. agony 4. puff 5. wane 6. coma 7. bubble 8. beneficent 9. curse 10. rally 11. perspire 12. justify 13. repletion

C. 직독직해

아래에 제시된 문장을 직독직해로 해석해보세요.

1. A son / who would come there / after he was gone / -a son / who would stand proud and strong / before some subsequent Stuffy, / and say: "In memory of my father."

    →

2. He intended to speak; / and as the Old Gentleman had heard / the sounds nine times before, / he rightly construed / them into Stuffy's old way of acceptance.

    →

3. He saw the look / of beneficent happiness / on the Old Gentleman's face / -a happier look / than even a flower or a strange butterfly had ever brought to it / -and he had not the heart to see / it wane.

    →

4. There was no smell of whiskey / to justify a transfer / to the patrol wagon, / so Stuffy and his two dinners went to the hospital.

    →

D. 동시통역

아래에 제시된 직독직해를 보고, 영어로 말해보세요.

1. 이것이 늙은 신사가 말하는 것이었다 / 매번

    →

2. 그들은 알려졌다 / 이 식당에서

    →

3. 한 시간 후에 스터피는 (의자에) 기대었다 / 전투에서 이기고

    →

4. 1시간 후에 또 다른 앰뷸런스가 데려왔다 / 그 늙은 신사를

    →

Answer

C. 1. 아들을 (바랬다) / 여기에 올 / 그가 죽은 뒤에 / 아들을 (바랬다) / 자랑스러워하고 그리고 당당하게 행동하는 / 스터피의 뒤를 잇는 인물 앞에서 / 그리고 말할 수 있는 (아들): "아버지를 기념하며"라고 2. 어떤 말을 하려고 했다 / 그리고 늙은 신사가 들었기 때문에 / (스피트의) 소리를 예전에 9번이나 / 그는 바로 해석했다 / 그 소리를 (식사대접을) 스터피가 수락하는 일상적인 (표현) 방법으로 3. 그는 표정을 봤다 / 인자하고 행복한 / 늙은 신사의 얼굴에서 / 더 행복한 표정이었다 / 꽃이나 진귀한 나비가 가져다 준 것보다 더 (행복한) / 그리고 스터피는 볼 용기가 없었다 / 그 행복이 사라지는 것을 4. 술 냄새가 나지 않았다 / 인계하는 것을 정당화시킬 수 있을 정도로 / 경찰의 범인 호송차로 / 그래서 스터피와 두 번 먹은 저녁식사는 병원으로 갔다

D. 1. That is what the old Gentleman said / every time. 2. They were known / at this place. 3. In an hour Stuffy leaned back / with a battle won. 4. An hour later another ambulance brought / the Old Gentleman.

A Retrieved Reformation
개과천선

SCENE 1

A guard came to the prison shoe-shop, /
간수가 교도소 내의 구두 가게로 왔다 /

where Jimmy Valentine was assiduously stitching uppers, /
그곳에서 지미 발렌타인이 부지런히 구두의 윗부분을 꿰매고 있었다 /

and escorted / him to the prison office.
그리고 데리고 갔다 / 지미를 교도소 사무실로

There the warden handed / Jimmy his pardon, /
거기서 교도소장이 건네주었다 / 지미에게 사면장을 /

which had been signed / that morning by the governor.
그 사면장은 서명되어 있었다 / 그날 아침 주지사에 의해

Jimmy took it / in a tired kind of way.
지미는 그것을 받았다 / 지친 듯이

He had served nearly ten months /
그는 거의 10개월을 복역한 상태였다 /

of a four year sentence. He had expected to stay /
4년형을 선고 받고 그는 (교도소에) 머무를 것으로 예상했었다 /

only about three months, / at the longest.
겨우 3개월 정도 / 기껏해야

Jimmy Valentine had many influential friends /
지미 발렌타인은 많은 영향력 있는 친구가 있었다 /

outside the prison.
감옥 바깥세상에

It is hardly worth his while to cut his hair.
(그래서) 그가 머리를 깎을 필요도 없다(머리를 깎을 필요도 없이 금방 나간다)

"Now, Valentine," said the warden,
자 발렌타인 교도소장이 말했다

"you'll go out in the morning.
넌 아침에 출소할 거야

Brace up, / and make a man of yourself.
기운을 내서 / 착한 사람이 되라고

110 O. Henry's Short Stories

You're not a bad fellow at heart.
너는 심성이 나쁜 친구는 아니야.

Stop cracking safes, and live straight."
금고 터는 일은 그만하고 똑바로 살아

"Me?" said Jimmy, in surprise.
제가요? 지미가 놀래서 말했다

"Why, I never cracked a safe / in my life."
뭐요, 저는 한번도 금고를 턴 적이 없어요 / 태어나서

"Oh, no," laughed the warden.
오, 아니라고 교도소장이 웃었다

"Of course not. Let's see, now.
물론 그렇겠지 자 보라고

How was it / you happened to get sent to prison /
어째서 / 너는 감옥에 오게 됐지 /

on that Springfield job?
스프링필드에서 도둑질한 사건으로

Was it because you wouldn't prove an alibi /
(네가 옥살이를 한 이유가) 네 알리바이를 증명하지 않았기 때문이냐 /

for fear of compromising somebody / in high society?
누군가의 명예에 손상을 입힐까봐 / 품위 있는 상류사회의

Or was it simply a case of a mean old jury /
아니면 단순하게 비열하고 늙은 배심원 때문에 발생한 사건이냐 /

that had it in for you?
너에게 원한을 품은

You men always have a reason / like that.
너희 같은 사람들은 늘 이유가 있지 / 그와 같은

You never went to prison / if you didn't crack a safe.
절대로 교도소에 오지 않았을 것이야 / 네가 금고를 털지 않았다면

"Me?" said Jimmy, still blankly innocent.
제가요? 지미는 말했다 여전히 완전히 아무 죄가 없듯이

"Why, warden, I never was in Springfield / in my life!"
아니, 교도소장님 저는 스프링필드에 가본 적이 없다니까요 / 태어나서

---

assiduously 부지런히 upper (구두의) 윗부분 escort 호송하다, 데리고 가다 warden 교도소장 pardon 사면장 governor 주지사 serve 복역하다 sentence (법정에 의해 선고된) 형, 형벌 influential 영향력 있는 crack 부수다 alibi 알리바이 compromise (신용, 명예를) 떨어뜨리다, 손상시키다 society 상류사회 case 사건

"Take him back, Cronin!" said the warden,
이 자를 데려가 크로닌   교도소장이 말했다

"and give him outgoing clothes.
그리고 그에게 출소 복을 줘

Unlock him at seven in the morning,
아침 7시에 문을 열어줘,

and let him come to the bull-pen.
그리고 유치장으로 보내

Better think over / my advice, Valentine."
잘 생각해봐 /   내 충고를, 발렌타인

bull-pen (속어) 유치장

SCENE 2

At a quarter past seven / on the next morning /
7시 15분에 / 다음날 아침

Jimmy stood / in the warden's outer office.
지미는 서있었다 / 교도소장의 바깥쪽 사무실에

He had on / a suit of the non-matching,
그는 입고 있었고 / 한 벌의 몸에 맞지 않는

ready-made clothes /
기성복을 /

and a pair of the stiff, / squeaky shoes /
그리고 한 켤레의 뻣뻣한 / 삐걱거리는 신발을 신고 /

that the state furnishes /
(그 옷과 신발을) 주 정부는 주는 /

to its discharged compulsory guests.
석방되는 강제로 수용한 손님들에게

The clerk handed him /
직원이 지미에게 건넸다 /

a railroad ticket and the five-dollar bill / with which /
기차표 한 장과 5달러짜리 지폐를 / 그 기차표와 돈으로 /

the law expected / him to rehabilitate himself /
법을 집행하는 기관은 기대했다 / 그가 돌아가길 /

into good citizenship and prosperity.
선량한 시민과 번영으로

The warden gave him a cigar, / and shook hands.
교도소장은 그에게 시가를 한 개 주고 나서 / 악수를 했다

Valentine, 9762, was chronicled / on the books, /
발렌타인은, 죄수번호가 9762인 기입되었다 / 죄수 명부에 /

"Pardoned by Governor," /
"주지사에 의한 사면" 이라고 /

and Mr. James Valentine walked out /
그리고 제임스 발렌타인은 걸어 나왔다 /

into the sunshine.
햇살 속으로

Disregarding the song of the birds,
(무시하면서) 새들의 노랫소리,

the waving green trees, and the smell of the flowers, /
물결치는 푸른 나무들, 그리고 꽃 냄새를 무시하면서 /

Jimmy headed straight / for a restaurant.
지미는 곧장 향했다 / 식당으로

There he tasted / the first sweet joys of liberty /
거기서 그는 맛보았다 / 자유의 첫 번째 달콤한 기쁨을 /

in the shape of a broiled chicken and a bottle of white wine
(어떻게 맛보았는가?) 통닭구이 한 마리와 백포도주 한 병

-followed by a cigar / a grade better /
그리고 시가 한개를 즐기는(형식으로) / (그 시가는) 한 등급 더 좋은 /

than the one the warden had given him.
교도소장이 주었던 것보다

From there he proceeded leisurely to the depot.
식당에서 그는 느긋하게 기차역으로 갔다

He tossed a quarter / into the hat of a blind man /
그는 25센트 동전을 던졌다 / 시각장애인의 모자 속으로 /

sitting by the door, / and boarded his train.
문 옆에 앉아있는 / 그리고는 기차에 탔다

Three hours set him down in a little town /
3시간 걸려서 그는 작은 마을에 도착했다 /

near the state line.
주 경계선에 가까이 있는

He went to the cafe of Mike Dolan /
그는 마이크 돌런의 카페로 가서 /

and shook hands with Mike,
마이크와 악수를 했다 /

who was alone behind the bar.
(그리고 마이크는) 혼자 카운터 뒤에 있었다

---

a suit of 한 벌의 non-matching 어울리지 않는 squeaky 삐걱거리는 furnish 주다 discharge 석방하다 compulsory 강제적인 the law 법을 집행하는 기관, 경찰 rehabilitate (사람을) 사회로 복귀시키다, (사람을 건강한 상태로) 돌아가게 하다 prosperity 번영, 성공 chronicle 연대순으로 기록하다 book 명부, 장부 pardon 사면하다 disregard 무시하다 in the shape of ~의 형식으로 broil 굽다 depot 기차역, 정거장 board 승차하다, 타다

SCENE 3

"Sorry we couldn't do it sooner,
미안해 좀 더 빨리 꺼내주지 못해서,

Jimmy, my boy," said Mike.
이봐, 지미 마이크가 말했다

"But we had that protest from Springfield /
그러나 우리는 스프링필드에서 반대가 있었지 /

to buck against, / and the governor nearly balked.
완강하게 저항하는 / 그리고 주지사가 하마터면 안 해줄 뻔했어

Feeling all right?" "Fine," said Jimmy. "Got my key?"
기분은 어때? 좋아 지미가 말했다 내 열쇠 갖고 있어?

He got his key and went upstairs, /
지미는 열쇠를 갖고 위층으로 올라갔다 /

unlocking the door of a room / at the rear.
방의 문을 열었다 / 뒤쪽에 있는

Everything was just / as he had left it.
모든 것이 그대로였다 / 그가 떠날 때와 마찬가지로

There on the floor was still / Ben Price's collar-button /
마루에는 아직도 있었다 / 벤 프라이스의 (코트) 칼라 단추가 /

that had been torn / from that eminent detective's coat /
(그 단추는) 떨어졌었던 / 유명한 형사의 코트에서 /

when they had overpowered Jimmy / to arrest him.
그들이 지미를 제압했을 때 / 지미를 체포하려고

Pulling out from the wall / a folding-bed, /
벽에서 꺼내고 나서 / 접어 넣는 간이침대를 /

Jimmy slid back / a panel in the wall /
지미는 밀어 넣고 / 벽의 널빤지 한 장을 /

and dragged out a dust-covered suit-case.
그리고 먼지가 쌓인 여행 가방을 꺼냈다

He opened this and gazed fondly /
여행 가방을 열고 사랑스럽게 바라보았다 /

at the finest set of burglar's tools / in the East.
밤도둑의 가장 훌륭한 연장 세트를 / 동부지역에서

---

buck against 완강하게 저항하다 balk 망설이다, 주저하다, 시도하지 않다 unlock 자물쇠로 열다 rear 뒤쪽
eminent 유명한 overpower 눌러 복종케 하다, 제압하다

It was a complete set, /
그것은 완전한 풀 세트였다 /

made of specially tempered steel /
특별히 단련된 강철로 만들어졌고 /

in various shapes and sizes, /
여러 종의 모양과 크기로 /

invented by Jimmy himself, / in which he took pride.
지미가 직접 발명했던 /   (그리고 이 연장 세트를) 지미가 자랑스럽게 생각했다

Over nine hundred dollars they had cost him /
900달러 이상의 비용이 들었다 /

to have made / at a place where they make such things /
이것들을 만드는데 /   이런 것들을 만들어 주는 모처에서 /

for the safebreaking profession.
금고털이 직종을 위해

In half an hour Jimmy went down stairs /
30분 뒤에 지미는 아래층으로 내려가서 /

and through the cafe. He was now dressed /
카페를 빠져(나갔다)   그는 이제 입었다 /

in tasteful and well-fitting clothes, / and carried /
세련되고 몸에 잘 맞는 옷을 /   그리고 운반했다 /

his dusted and cleaned suit-case / in his hand.
먼지를 털어 깨끗한 여행 가방을 /   손으로

Key Expression

대명사는 무엇을 가리키는가?

It(the set of burglar's tools) was a complete set, /
그것(밤도둑의 연장 세트)은 완전한 풀 세트였다 /
*대명사(it)를 보면, 어떤 것(the set of burglar's tools)을 가리키는지 알아본다.

made of specially tempered steel / in various shapes and sizes, /
(그리고 그 연장 세트는) 특별히 단련된 강철로 만들어졌고 / 여러 종의 모양과 크기로 /
*"made"의 주어는 "the set of burglar's tools"(밤도둑의 연장 세트)이다.

invented by Jimmy himself, /
(그리고 그 연장 세트는) 지미가 직접 발명했다 /
*"invented"의 주어도 "the set of burglar's tools"(밤도둑의 연장 세트)이다.

in which he took pride.
(그래서 이 연장 세트에) 지미는 자부심을 느낀다.
"which"는 "a complete set"를 가리킨다.

---

temper (강철을) 단련하다 tasteful 세련된 dust 먼지를 털다

SCENE 4

"Do you have anything on?" asked Mike Dolan, / genially.
펠 하려고 해   마이크 돌런이 물어봤다 /   상냥하게

"Me?" said Jimmy, / in a puzzled tone.
나?   지미가 말했다 /   당황한 말투로

"I don't understand. I work for /
무슨 말인지 모르겠는데   나는 직원이야 /

the New York Biscuit Cracker and cake Company.
뉴욕 비스킷 크래커 케익 회사의

And I sell / the best cracker and cake / in the country."
그리고 나는 팔아 /   최고의 크래커와 케이크를 /   이 나라에서

This statement delighted Mike / to such an extent /
이 말이 마이크를 기쁘게 했다 /   매우

that Jimmy had to take a drink / with him on the spot.
그래서 지미는 한 잔 마시게 되었다 /   마이크와 즉석에서

He never touched / "hard" drinks.
지미는 마시지 않았다 /   도수가 높은 술을

A week / after the release of Valentine, 9762, /
1주일이 지나자 / 죄수번호 9762번인 발렌타인을 석방한 지 /

there was a neat job of safe-burglary /
말끔한 솜씨의 금고털이 사건이 있었다 /

done in Richmond, Indiana,
인디애나 주 리치몬드에서 발생한 /

with no clue / who did it.
실마리를 남기지 않고 / 누가 범인인지

A scant eight hundred dollars was taken.
얼마 안 되는 800불만 도난당했다

Two weeks after that /
그 사건이후 2주 후에 /

a patented, improved, burglar-proof safe /
특허를 받고, 개량된 도난방지 금고가 /

in Logansport / was opened like a cheese.
로간스포트에 있던 /   치즈처럼 열렸다

---

genially 상냥하게 delight 기쁘게 하다 scant 부족한, 적은 patented 특허를 받은 burglar-proof 도난 방지의

Fifteen hundred dollars in cash were taken,
1,500불이나 현찰로 도난당했다 /

securities and silver untouched.
증권과 은화는 손을 대지 않았다

That began to interest / the detectives.
이것이 관심을 끌기 시작했다 / 형사들의

Then an old-fashioned bank-safe in Jefferson City was
그 후에 제퍼슨 시에 있는 구닥다리의 은행금고가 열렸고 /

opened / and bank-notes amounting to five thousand
그리고 5천 달러에 달하는 지폐가 도난당했다

dollars were taken.

The losses were now high enough / to bring the matter up /
피해액이 이제 충분히 커졌다 / 그 사건이 끌어들일 정도로 /

into Ben Price's class of work.
벤 프라이스 형사와 같은 급의 활동을

By comparing notes, / a remarkable similarity /
의견을 교환해보니 / 매우 유사한 점이 /

in the methods of the burglaries / was noticed.
강도질하는 방법에서 / 발견되었다

Ben Price investigated / the scenes of the robberies, /
벤 프라이스는 조사했고 / 도난현장을 /

and was heard to remark:
(소문에 의하면 아래와 같이) 의견을 말했다고 한다

"That's Dandy Jim Valentine's autograph.
이건 멋쟁이 짐 발렌타인의 자필 서명이야(그가 한 짓이야)

He's resumed business.
그가 다시 일을 시작했군

Look at that combination knob / -jerked out as easy /
비밀번호 손잡이를 봐 / 쉽게 비틀어 빠진 /

as pulling up a radish in wet weather.
비오는 날 무를 뽑아내듯이

Only he's got the tools / that can do it.
그만이 장비를 갖고 있지 / (어떤 장비?) 저런 일을 할 수 있는

And look / how clean those tumblers were punched out!
그리고 보라고 / 얼마나 깨끗하게 자물쇠의 회전판이 구멍이 뚫렸나!

Jimmy never has to drill but one hole.
지미는 항상 구멍을 한 개만 뚫어

Yes, I want Mr. Valentine.
그래, 발렌타인을 잡자

He'll do his bit next time /
그는 다음번에는 형기를 채우게 될 거야 /

without any short-time or clemency foolishness."
단기 형이나 사면 같이 터무니없는 일 없이

Key Expression

have ~on

1. ~을 계획(예정)하고 있다
   Do you have anything on for Christmas?
   너는 어떤 계획이 있니 / 크리스마스 때
2. ~를 입고 있다, 착용하고 있다
   She has on long gloves. 그녀는 끼고 있다 / 긴 장갑을
3. (나쁜 짓을) 알고 있다
   What did the police have on Valentine?
   어떤 나쁜 짓을 경찰은 알고 있나 / 발렌타인에 대해

---

securities 유가증권 bank-note 지폐 amount to (액수가) ~에 이르다 compare notes 정보(의견)를 교환하다
similarity 유사(점) burglary 강도, 불법침입 robbery 강도, 도난 dandy 멋쟁이 autograph 자필 서명
resume 다시 시작하다 combination knob 비밀번호 손잡이 jerk out 쑥쑥 뽑다 tumbler 자물쇠의 회전판
clemency (재판이나 처벌의) 관용, 사면

SCENE 5

Ben Price knew / Jimmy's habits.
벤 프라이스는 알고 있다 / 지미의 버릇을

He had learned them / while working on the Springfield case.
그는 지미의 버릇을 알게 되었다 / (언제?) 스프링필드 사건을 조사할 때

Long escapes, quick get-aways, no accomplices,
장거리 도피, 빠른 도주, 공모자가 없고,

and a taste for good society / -these ways had helped /
상류 사회 생활에 대한 취미 / 이러한 것들은 도움이 되었다 /

Mr. Valentine to become noted /
발렌타인을 유명하게 하는데 /

as a successful dodger of retribution.
벌을 잘 피하는 사람으로

It was widely known / that Ben Price had taken up the trail /
널리 알려 졌다 / (어떤 일이?) 벤 프라이스가 뒤를 쫓기 시작했다는 것이 /

of the elusive cracksman, / and other people /
교묘히 피하는 금고털이범의 / 그러자 다른 사람들은 /

with burglar-proof safes / felt more at ease.
도난방지 금고를 가진 / 좀 더 마음이 편해졌다

One afternoon Jimmy Valentine and his suit-case climbed
어느 오후에 지미 발렌타인과 그의 여행 가방은 내려졌다 /

out of / the mail coach / in Elmore, / a small town,
우편물 마차에서 / 엘모어라는 곳의 / (엘모어는) 작은 마을인 /

Arkansas. / Jimmy, / looking like an athletic senior /
아칸소 주에 있는 지미는 / 4학년 운동선수처럼 보였던 /

just home from college, / went down the board side-walk /
대학에서 방금 집으로 온 / 널빤지를 깐 보도를 걸어서 갔다 /

toward the hotel. A young lady crossed the street, /
호텔을 향해서 한 젊은 숙녀가 거리를 건넜고 /

passed him / at the corner / and entered a door /
지미를 지나쳤다 / 모퉁이에서 / 그리고 입구로 들어갔다 /

over which was the sign, / "The Elmore Bank."
(그 입구 위에) 간판이 있었던 / '엘모어 은행' 이라고 쓰인

Jimmy Valentine looked into her eyes, /
지미 발렌타인은 그녀의 눈을 들여다보고 /

forgot what he was, / and became another man.
자신이 뭘 하는 인간인지 잊었으며 / 다른 사람이 되어 버렸다

She lowered her eyes / and had red cheeks.
그녀는 눈을 내리깔았고 / 볼이 약간 불그스름해졌다

Young men of Jimmy's style and looks were scarce /
지미와 같은 스타일과 외모의 젊은이가 드물었다 /

in Elmore. Jimmy collared a boy / that was loafing /
엘모어에서는 지미는 한 소년을 붙잡았다 / (어떤 소년?) 빈둥거리고 있던 /

on the steps of the bank / as if he were one of the
은행의 계단에서 / 마치 자신이 주주중의 한 명인 것처럼 /

stockholders, / and began to ask him questions /
그리고 소년에게 물어보기 시작했다 /

about the town, / handing him dimes / at intervals.
마을에 대해서 / 10센트짜리 동전을 주면서 / 가끔씩

By and by the young lady came out, / looking unconscious /
잠시 후 그 젊은 숙녀가 나왔다 / 의식하지 않는 모습으로 /

of the young man with the suit-case, / and went her way.
여행 가방을 든 젊은 남자를 / 그리고 갈 길을 갔다

"Isn't that young lady Polly Simpson?" asked Jimmy, /
저 젊은 숙녀가 폴리 심슨이니? 지미가 물었다 /

with specious guile.
그럴듯한 꾀를 부려

Key Expression

take up

1. (중단된 활동을) 다시 시작하다
   Let's take up the discussion. 토론을 다시 시작하자.
2. ~을 취미로 시작하다
   She took up painting when she moved to suburbs.
   그녀는 취미로 그림을 그리기 시작했다 / 그녀가 교외로 이사 갔을 때
3. (위치를) 차지하다
   I took up the best position to watch people fighting on the street.
   나는 가장 좋은 자리를 차지했다 / 구경하려고 / 사람들이 싸우는 것을 / 길거리에서

accomplice 공모자 noted 유명한 dodger 몸을 피하는 사람 retribution (나쁜 짓에 대한) 벌, 응보
take up 시작하다 trail 추적, 추적하는 일, 흔적 elusive 교묘히 피하는 side-walk 보도 collar ~을 붙잡다
loaf 빈둥거리다 stockholder 주주 interval (시간의) 간격, 사이 at intervals 가끔씩, 이따금
unconscious 의식하지 않은 specious 그럴듯한 guile 교활한 꾀

SCENE 6

"No," said the boy.
아니요 소년이 말했다

"She's Annabel Adams. Her father owns this bank.
저 여자는 애너벨 아담스예요   그녀의 아버지가 이 은행 주인이죠

What did you come to Elmore for?
엘모어에는 왜 오셨어요?

Is that a gold watch-chain?
이것이 금 시곗줄 인가요?

I'm going to get a bulldog. Got any more dimes?"
저는 불독 한 마리를 사려고 해요.   10센트짜리 동전 더 있어요?

Jimmy went to the Planters' Hotel, /
지미는 플렌터스 호텔로 가서 /

registered as Ralph D. Spencer, / and engaged a room.
랠프 D. 스펜서라는 이름으로 숙박부에 기입하고 /   방을 예약했다

He leaned on the desk and / he told the clerk /
그는 프론트 데스크에 기대고 서서   그는 호텔 직원에게 말했다 /

he had come to Elmore / to look for a location /
그는 엘모어에 왔다고 /   (왜?) 장소를 물색하기 위해서 /

to go into business. How was the shoe business, now,
(어떤 장소?) 사업을 할 만한   신발 장사가 어떤지?   현재

in the town? He had thought of the shoe business.
마을에서   그는 신발 장사에 대해 생각해본 적이 있었다

Was there already a shoe-shop?
이미 구둣가게가 있는가?

The clerk was impressed /
호텔 직원은 좋은 인상을 받았다 /

by the clothes and manner of Jimmy.
지미의 옷차림과 매너에서

He was something of a pattern of fashion /
그 호텔 직원은 패션에 본보기가 되는 존재였다 /

to the youth of Elmore, / but he now perceived /
엘모어의 젊은이들에게 /   그러나 그는 지금은 알아차렸다 /

his shortcomings.
자신의 단점을

While trying to figure out / Jimmy's manner of tying his
호텔 직원이 알아내려고 했을 때 / 지미가 일반적인 넥타이를 매는 방법을 /

four-in-hand / he cordially gave information.
지미는 공손하게 가르쳐 주었다

Yes, there must be a good opening / in the shoe line.
그렇다, 좋은 기회가 있음에 틀림없다 / 구두 장사에

There wasn't an exclusive shoe-store / in the place.
구두만 파는 가게가 하나도 없었다 / 이 지역에는

The dry-goods and general stores handled them.
포목 가게와 잡화 가게에서 신발을 취급하고 있었다(팔고 있었다)

Business in all lines / was fairly good.
어떤 업종의 사업을 하든지 / 아주 괜찮았다

He hoped / Mr. Spencer would decide to stay / in Elmore.
그는 바랬다 스펜서씨가 자리 잡기로 결정하길 / 엘모어에

He would find / it a pleasant town to live in, /
그는 알게 될 것이다 / 이곳(엘모어)이 살기에 좋은 마을이라는 것을 /

and the people very sociable.
그리고 사람들도 아주 사교적이라는 것을 (알게 될 것이었다)

Mr. Spencer thought / he would stop over /
스펜서씨는 생각했다 / 그는 머무르겠다고 /

in the town a few days / and look over the situation.
마을에 며칠동안 / 그리고 상황을 살펴보겠다고 (생각했다)

No, the clerk needn't call the boy.
아니, 직원이 보이를 부를 필요가 없었다.

He would carry up his suit-case, / himself; /
그(지미)는 들고 갈 것이었다 / 여행 가방을 / 직접

it was rather heavy.
(왜냐하면) 그 가방은 좀 무거웠다

Mr. Ralph Spencer, / the phoenix /
랠프 스펜서라는 사람은 / 불사조로서 / (어떤 불사조?)

that arose from Jimmy Valentine's ashes /
지미 발렌타인의 잿더미에서 날아오른 /

remained in Elmore, and prospered.
엘모어에 남았고 번성했다.(과거 생활을 청산하고 랠프 스펜서로 새롭게 태어났다)

He opened a shoe-store / and business was good.
구두 가게를 하나 내었고 / 장사가 잘 되었다

register 기록하다, 등록하다 engage 예약하다 perceive 지각하다, 알아차리다 shortcoming 단점
four-in-hand (Y자 모양의) 매듭 넥타이 cordially 공손하게 exclusive ~전용의, 독점적인
dry-goods 포목, 직물 line 사업, 업종

Quiz 8

A. 내용 이해하기

다음 문장을 읽고 본문의 내용과 맞으면 T(True), 틀리면 F(False)를 쓰세요.

1. Jimmy was given a pardon because it was proved he did not have committed a crime.
2. Jimmy went to his friend's cafe to take his set of tools as soon as he was released.
3. Jimmy changed his name to break safes in Elmore.
4. Jimmy fell in love with a banker's daughter at first sight.

B. 단어

다음 제시된 단어의 설명을 읽고, 어떤 단어의 정의를 설명하는지 아래의 박스에서 찾아서 보세요.

1. a person who is in charge of the political administration of a state in the United States
2. to pass time not doing anything
3. to be unwilling to do or try something
4. punishment for a crime
5. different from the usual way in which something can be done
6. a person who helps a law-breaker to commit a crime
7. well-known and respected; famous
8. to restore a healthy, useful life again after they have been in prison
9. a man who always cares a great deal about his appearance and clothes
10. less severe punishment for a crime; willingness not to punish somebody severely
11. to provide something with somebody

> governor rehabilitate balk eminent dandy clemency accomplice
> furnish retribution loaf alternative

Answer A. 1. F 2. T 3. F 4. T
B. 1. governor 2. loaf 3. balk 4. retribution 5. alternative 6. accomplice 7. eminent 8. rehabilitate 9. dandy
10. clemency 11. furnish

C. 직독직해

아래에 제시된 문장을 직독직해로 해석해보세요.

1. The clerk handed him / a railroad ticket and the five-dollar bill / with which / the law expected / him to rehabilitate himself / into good citizenship and prosperity.

   →

2. It was a complete set, / made of specially tempered steel / in various shapes and sizes, / invented by Jimmy himself, / in which he took pride.

   →

3. It was widely known / that Ben Price had taken up the trail / of the elusive cracksman, / and other people / with burglar-proof safes / felt more at ease.

   →

4. Jimmy Valentine looked into her eyes, / forgot what he was, / and became another man.

   →

D. 동시통역

아래에 제시된 직독직해를 보고, 영어로 말해보세요.

1. 그는 거의 10개월을 복역한 상태였다 / 4년형을 선고 받고

   →

2. 30분 뒤에 지미는 아래층으로 내려가서 / 카페를 빠져(나갔다)

   →

3. 그것이 관심을 끌기 시작했다 / 형사들의

   →

4. 어떤 업종의 사업을 하든지 / 아주 괜찮았다.

   →

Answer

C. 1. 직원이 지미에게 건넸다 / 기차표 한 장과 5달러짜리 지폐를 / 그 기차표와 돈으로 / 법을 집행하는 기관은 기대했다 / 그가 돌아가길 / 선량한 시민과 번영으로 2. 그것은 완전한 풀 세트였다 / 특별히 단련된 강철로 만들어졌고 / 여러 종의 모양과 크기로 / 지미가 직접 발명했다 / (그리고 이 연장 세트를) 지미가 자랑스럽게 생각했다 3. 널리 알려 졌다 / (어떤 일이?) 벤 프라이스가 뒤를 쫓기 시작했다는 것이 / 교묘히 피하는 금고털이의 / 그러자 다른 사람들은 / 도난방지 금고를 가진 / 좀 더 마음이 편해졌다. 4. 지미 발렌타인은 그녀의 눈을 들여다보고 / 자신이 뭘 하는 인간인지 잊었으며 / 다른 사람이 되어 버렸다.

D. 1. He had served nearly ten months / of a four year sentence. 2. In half an hour Jimmy went down stairs / and through the cafe. 3. That began to interest / the detectives. 4. Business in all lines / was fairly good.

SCENE 7

Socially he was also a success, / and made many friends.
사회적으로도 그는 성공한 사람이 되었고 / 많은 친구를 사귀었다

And he accomplished / the wish of his heart.
그리고 그는 이루었다 / 마음속의 소원을

He met Miss Annabel Adams, / and became more and
그는 애너벨 아담스를 만났고 / 점점 더 빠져들었다 /

more captivated / by her charms.
그녀의 매력에

At the end of a year / the situation of Mr. Ralph Spencer
1년이 지났을 때 / 랠프 스펜서의 상황은 다음과 같았다 /

was this: / he had won the respect of the community, /
그는 지역 사회의 신임을 얻었고 /

his shoe-store was flourishing, / and he and Annabel were
구두 가게는 번창했었고 / 그리고 애너벨과 약혼했다 /

engaged / to be married / in two weeks.
결혼하기위하여 / 2주 후에

Mr. Adams, the typical, plodding, country banker, /
아담스씨는 전형적인 노력형의 시골 은행가인 /

approved of Spencer.
스펜서를 마음에 들어 했다

Annabel's pride in him / almost equalled her affection.
그에 대한 애너벨의 자부심과 / 거의 그녀의 사랑은 같았다

He was as much at home / in the family of Mr. Adams /
그는 마음 편하게 지냈다 / 아담스씨의 집에서나 /

and that of Annabel's married sister /
애너벨의 결혼한 언니의 집에서나 /

as if he were already a member.
마치 그가 벌써 (가족의) 일원이 된 것처럼

One day Jimmy sat down in his room / and wrote this letter, /
어느날 지미는 그의 방에 앉아서 / 이 편지를 썼다 /

which he mailed / to the safe address /
(그러고 나서 그 편지를) 그는 보냈다 / 안전한 주소로 /

of one of his old friends / in St. Louis:
옛날 친구들 중 한 명의 / 세인트 루이스에 있는

Dear Old Pal:
그리운 친구에게

I want / you to be at Sullivan's place, / in Little Rock, /
나는 바래 / 네가 설리번의 집으로 와주길 / 리틀락에 있는 /

next Wednesday night, at nine o'clock.
다음주 수요일 밤 9시에

I want / you to wind up / some little matters for me.
나는 바래 / 네가 마무리 해 주길 / 나를 위해 사소한 문제를

And, also, I want to / make you a present / of my kit of tools.
그리고 또 나는 원해 / 너에게 선물로 주길 / 내 연장을

I know / you'll be glad / to get them /
난 알아 / 네가 좋아할 것이란 걸 / 그걸 받으면 /

-you couldn't duplicate them / for a thousand dollars.
너는 그것과 똑같이 만들 수 없어 / 1천 달러를 줘도

Say, Billy, I've quit the old business-a year ago.
그런데 빌리, 나는 예전에 하던 사업을 그만뒀어-1년 전에

I've got a nice store.
나는 근사한 가게를 하나 갖고 있어

I'm making an honest living, / and I'm going to marry /
나는 정직하게 살고 있어 / 그리고 결혼할 예정이야 /

the finest girl on earth / two weeks from now.
세상에서 제일 좋은 여자와 / 지금으로부터 2주 후에

It's the only life, Billy -the straight one.
이것이 유일한 삶이야 빌리 -정직한 삶만이

I wouldn't touch a dollar / of another man's money /
나는 1달러도 손대지 않아 / 남의 돈의 /

now for a million.
이젠 1백만 달러를 줘도

After I get married / I'm going to sell out and go West, /
결혼한 다음에는 / 가게를 팔고 서부로 갈 거야 /

where there won't be so much danger / of seeing anyone /
그곳에는 위험이 없을 거야 / 누군가를 만날 /

who knew me in my old life.
과거의 나를 알고 있는

accomplish 이루다 captivate 마음을 사로잡다 charm 매력 flourish 번창하다 plodding 꾸준히 일하는
affection 사랑, 애정 pal 친구 wind up (일, 문제를) 마무리하다, 정리하다 duplicate 복제하다

I tell you, Billy, she's an angel.
빌리, 내 신부는 천사야

She believes in me; / and I wouldn't do another crooked
그녀는 날 믿어 /   그리고 나는 부정직한 짓은 안할 거야 /

thing / for the whole world.
무슨 일이 있어도

Be sure to be at Sully's, / for I must see you.
설리번의 집에 꼭 와줘 /   왜냐하면 나는 널 꼭 봐야하니까

I'll bring along the tools with me.
연장은 내가 갖고 갈게

Your old friend,
오랜 친구

Jimmy.
지미

Key Expression

동사의 쓰임새 익히기

1. approve of; ~을 마음에 들어 하다, 좋다고 생각하다

   My parents approved of my marrying her.
   내 부모님들은 마음에 들어 하지 않았다 / 내가 그녀와 결혼하는 것을
   She doesn't approve of cosmetic surgery.
   그녀는 좋다고 생각하지 않는다 / 성형수술을

2. approve + 목적어; ~을 승인하다, 가결하다, 찬성하다

   The National Assembly approved the bill by a vote of 50 to 45.
   국회는 가결했다 / 그 법안을 / 50대 45의 표차이로
   I don't approve your plan.
   나는 찬성하지 않아요 / 당신의 계획에

crooked 부정직한

SCENE 8

On the Monday night / after Jimmy wrote this letter, /
월요일 밤에 / 지미가 이 편지를 쓴 다음 /

Ben Price jogged quietly into Elmore / in a buggy.
벤 프라이스가 조심스럽게 천천히 엘모어로 왔다 / 마차를 타고

He lounged about town / in his quiet way /
그는 시내를 돌아봤다 / 조용히 /

until he found out / what he wanted to know.
그가 알아낼 때까지 / 알고 싶은 것을

From the drug-store / across the street from Spencer's
약국에서 / 스펜서의 구두 가게에서 거리 맞은편에 있는 /

shoe-store / he got a good look at Ralph D. Spencer.
그는 랠프 D. 스펜서를 자세히 봤다

"Are you going to marry the banker's daughter, Jimmy?"
은행가의 딸과 결혼한다고, 지미?

said Ben to himself.
벤이 중얼거렸다

"Well, I don't know!"
글쎄, 잘 될까!

The next morning Jimmy took breakfast / at the Adamses.
다음날 아침 지미는 아침을 먹었다 / 아담스씨 댁에서

He was going to Little Rock / that day to order his
그는 리틀 락으로 가려고 했다 / 그날 결혼 예복을 맞추려고 /

wedding-suit / and buy something nice / for Annabel.
그리고 근사한 것도 사려고 / 애너벨에게 줄

That would be the first time / he had left town /
이번이 처음이다 / 그가 마을을 떠나는 것은 /

since he came to Elmore.
그가 엘모어에 온 이래로

It had been more than a year now /
이제는 1년이 넘었다 /

since those last professional "jobs," /
그가 마지막으로 예전 일을 한 지 /

jog 말을 타고 느린 속도로 가다 buggy 4륜 경마차

and he thought / he could safely venture out.
그리고 그는 생각했다 / 위험을 무릅쓰고 안전하게 나갈 수 있다고

After breakfast / most of the Adams family went downtown
아침 식사 후 / 거의 모든 아담스 집안사람들은 번화가로 함께 갔다 /

together / -Mr. Adams, Annabel, Jimmy, and
- (집안사람들은) 아담스씨, 애너벨, 지미 그리고

Annabel's married sister with her two little girls, aged five
애너벨의 결혼한 언니와 5살과 9살 먹은 두 딸이(있었다)

and nine.

They came by the hotel / where Jimmy still boarded, /
그들은 호텔에 들렀다 / 그곳에 지미가 아직도 묵고 있었던 /

and he ran up to his room / and brought along his suit-case.
그리고 지미는 자기 방으로 올라가서 / 여행 가방을 갖고 왔다

Then they went on to the bank.
그 다음 그들은 은행으로 갔다

There stood / Jimmy's horse and buggy and Dolph Gibson, /
그곳에는 서있었다 / 지미의 말과 마차 그리고 돌프 깁슨이 /

who was going to drive him / over to the railroad station.
(그 돌프 깁슨은) 지미를 데려다 줄 것이다 / 기차역까지

All went / inside the high, carved oak railings /
모두가 들어갔다 / 높고 떡갈나무로 깎은 난간이 안쪽에 있는 /

into the banking-room / -Jimmy included, /
은행 사무실로 / - (사람들 속에) 지미도 포함되어 있었다 /

for Mr. Adams's future son-in-law / was welcome anywhere.
왜냐하면 아담스씨의 미래의 사위는 / 어디서나 환영받았기 때문이다

The clerks were pleased to be greeted /
은행 직원들은 인사 받는 것을 좋아했다 /

by the good-looking, agreeable young man /
잘 생기고 상냥한 젊은이한테 /

who was going to marry Miss Annabel.
(그 젊은이는) 애너벨 양과 결혼하게 되어 있는

Jimmy set his suit-case down. Annabel, / whose heart was
지미는 여행 가방을 내려놨다   애너벨은 /   그녀의 마음은 흥분하고 있었던 /

bubbling / with happiness and lively youth, /
   / 행복과 발랄한 젊음으로 /

---

venture 위험을 무릅쓰고 가다 railing 난간 agreeable 상냥한 bubble (기쁨으로) 흥분하다, 끓어오르다

put on Jimmy's hat, / and picked up the suit-case.
지미의 모자를 쓰고 / 여행 가방을 들어올렸다

"Wouldn't I make a nice salesperson?" said Annabel.
근사한 외판원 같지? 애너벨이 말했다

"My! Ralph, how heavy it is?
랠프, 뭐가 이렇게 무거워?

Feels like it was full / of gold bricks."
잔뜩 든 것 같아 / 금괴라도

SCENE 9

"Lot of nickel-plated shoe-horns in there," said Jimmy, / coolly, / "that I'm going to return.
Thought / I'd save express charges / by taking them up.
I'm getting awfully economical."

The Elmore Bank had just put in / a new safe.
Mr. Adams was very proud of it, / and insisted on / an inspection by every one.
The vault was a small one, / but it had a new, patented door.
It fastened / with three solid steel bolts / with a single handle, / and had a time-lock.
Mr. Adams beamingly explained / its workings / to Mr. Spencer, / who showed / a courteous interest / but not too intelligent one.
The two children, May and Agatha, were delighted / by the shining metal and funny lock and knobs.
While they were thus engaged / Ben Price sauntered in / and leaned on his elbow, /

looking casually inside / between the railings.
(그리고) 아무런 일이 없는 것처럼 안을 지켜보고 있었다 / 난간 사이로

He told the teller / that he didn't want anything; /
그는 은행 직원에게 말했다 / 그는 볼 일이 없다고 /

he was just waiting / for a man he knew.
그는 단지 기다리고 있다고(말했다) / 사람을 그가 아는

Suddenly there was a scream or two / from the women, /
갑자기 비명소리가 한두 번 들렸다 / 부인들 사이에서 /

and a commotion.
그리고 큰 소동이 (벌어졌다)

Unperceived by the elders,
어른들이 알아차리지 못하는 동안에(모르는 사이에)

May, / the nine-year-old girl, / in a spirit of play, /
메이가 / 9살 난 여자 아이였던 / 장난삼아 /

had shut Agatha / in the vault.
아가사를 가뒀다 / 금고실 안에

She had then closed / the door of the safe / and turned /
메이는 잠갔다 / 금고의 문을 / 그 다음에 돌려버렸다 /

the knob of the combination /
비밀번호를 맞추는 손잡이를 /

as she had seen / Mr. Adams do.
그녀가 보았던 대로 / 아담스씨가 하는 것을

The old banker sprang to the handle / and tugged at it /
늙은 은행가는 핸들로 뛰어갔고 / 핸들을 당겨보았다 /

for a moment.
잠시 동안

"The door can't be opened," he groaned.
문은 열 수가 없어 그가 신음했다

"The clock hasn't been wound / nor the combination set."
(시간 장치가 있는 자물쇠의) 태엽을 감지 않았고 / 비밀번호를 설정하지 않았어

Agatha's mother screamed again, / hysterically.
아가사의 엄마는 다시 비명을 질렀다 / 매우 흥분하여

---

plate ~을 도금하다 shoe-horn 구두주걱 economical 절약하는 insist on 주장하다 fasten 단단히 고정되다
courteous 정중한, 예의바른 intelligent 이해력이 빠른, 재치 있는 engaged 몰두하여, 바쁜
saunter 어슬렁어슬렁 걷다 commotion 동요, 소란 unperceived 알아차리지 못하는, 모르는 spirit 의도, 태도
combination 숫자의 조합 spring 뛰다, 덤벼들다 tug 당기다 groan 신음하다

SCENE 10

"Hush!" said Mr. Adams, / raising his trembling hand.
조용히 해! 아담스씨가 말했다 / 떨리는 손을 들면서

"All be quite for a moment. Agatha!" he called /
모두 잠시 조용히 하시오. 아가사! 그는 불렀다 /

as loudly as he could. "Listen to me."
있는 힘을 다해 큰 소리로 내 말소리가 들리니

During the following silence / they could just hear /
계속 이어지는 침묵 동안에 / 그들은 겨우 들을 수 있었다 /

the faint sound of the child /
희미한 아이의 소리를 /

wildly shrieking / in the dark vault / in a panic of terror.
(어떤 아이?) 마구 비명을 지르고 있었던 / 어두운 금고 속에서 / 공포 때문에 당황하여

"My precious darling!" wailed the mother.
내 아가! 엄마가 통곡했다

"She will die of fright! Open the door! Oh, break it open!
애가 무서워 죽을 거예요! 문을 열어요! 부셔서 열어요!

Can't you men do something?"
남자들이 어떻게 할 수 없어요?

"There isn't a man / nearer than Little Rock /
사람이 없다 / 리틀 락보다 가까운 곳에는(리틀 락까지 가야 사람을 찾을 수 있다)

who can open that door," / said Mr. Adams, /
(어떤 사람?) 이문을 열 수 있는 / 아담스씨가 말했다 /

in a shaky voice. "My God! Spencer, what shall we do?
떨리는 목소리로 맙소사! 스펜서, 어떻게 하지?

That child-she can't stand it / long in there.
저 애는 버티지 못해 / 오랫동안 저기서

There isn't enough air, / and, besides, /
공기도 충분하지 않고 / 게다가

she'll go into convulsions / from fright."
그녀는 경련을 일으킬 거야 / 놀래서

Agatha's mother, / frantic now, /
아가사의 엄마는 / 이제 미쳐서 /

beat the door of the vault / with her hands.
금고의 문을 때리고 있다 / 손으로

Somebody wildly suggested / dynamite.
누군가가 미친 듯이 제안했다 / 다이너마이트를 사용하자고

Annabel turned to Jimmy, /
애너벨은 지미 쪽으로 시선을 향했다(쳐다봤다) /

her large eyes full of anguish, / but not yet despairing.
그녀의 커다란 눈동자는 고뇌로 가득 찼지만 / 아직은 절망적이지 않았다

To a woman / nothing seems quite impossible /
여성이란 / 불가능해 보이는 것이 없는 것으로 안다 /

to the powers of the man / she worships.
남자의 힘에는 / (어떤 남자?) 자기가 존경하는

"Can't you do something, Ralph?"
어떻게 할 수 없어요, 랠프?

He looked at her / with a queer, soft smile /
그는 그녀를 쳐다봤다 / 기묘하고 부드러운 미소를 지으며 /

on his lips and in his keen eyes.
입술과 날카로운 눈에

"Annabel," he said, / "give me that rose / you are wearing,
애너벨 그가 말했다 / 그 장미를 줘봐 / 당신이 꽂고 있는,

will you?" Hardly believing / that she heard him rightly, /
응? 믿을 수 없었던(의심했지만) / 그녀가 똑바로 들었는지 /

she unpinned the bud / from the bosom of her dress, /
그녀는 핀에 꽂혀 있던 장미를 뺐고 / 드레스의 가슴부분에서 /

and placed it / in his hand.
장미를 놓았다 / 그의 손에

Jimmy stuffed it / into his vest-pocket, /
지미는 그것을 밀어 넣었다 / 조끼 주머니에 /

threw off his coat / and pulled up his shirt-sleeves.
코트를 벗었고 / 셔츠 소매를 걷어 올렸다

With that act / Ralph D. Spencer passed away /
그런 동작을 할 때 / 랠프 D. 스펜서는 사라졌고 /

and Jimmy Valentine took his place.
지미 발렌타인이 스펜서를 대신했다

"Get away from the door, all of you," he commanded,
문 앞에서 비켜나세요, 여러분 모두 그가 명령했다,

shortly.
간단하게

following 다음의 faint 희미한 shriek 비명을 지르다 wail 통곡하다 fright 공포 convulsion 경련
frantic 미친 turn to ~쪽으로 몸을 향하다 anguish 고뇌, 고민 despairing 절망적인 worship 존경하다
queer 기묘한 keen 날카로운 bud 활짝 피기전의 장미꽃 bosom 가슴(부분) vest-pocket 조끼의 주머니

SCENE 11

He set his suit-case on the table, / and opened it out flat.
그는 여행 가방을 테이블 위에 놓았고 / 그 가방을 열어 양쪽으로 펼쳤다

From that time on / he seemed to be unconscious /
그 순간부터 / 그는 의식하지 않는 것처럼 보였다 /

of the presence of any one else.
다른 사람이 존재하는 것을

He laid out / the shining, queer implements /
그는 꺼내 놓았다 / 빛나는 이상한 연장을 /

swiftly and orderly, / whistling softly to himself /
재빨리 그리고 질서 정연하게 / (그리고) 가볍게 휘파람을 불면서 /

as he always did / when at work.
언제나 그러하듯이 / 일할 때는

In a deep silence and immovable, / the others watched him /
깊은 침묵 속에서 움직이지 않았던 / 다른 사람들은 지미를 지켜봤다 /

as if under a spell. In a minute /
마치 마법에 걸린 듯이 1분 뒤에 /

Jimmy's pet drill was biting / smoothly into the steel door.
지미가 아끼는 드릴이 파고 들어갔다 / 부드럽게 강철 문을

In ten minutes / -breaking his own burglarious record- /
10분 후에는 / 그의 절도 기록을 깨뜨리고 /

he threw back the bolts / and opened the door.
그는 자물쇠 빗장을 들어 올리고 / 문을 열었다

Agatha, / almost collapsed, but safe, /
아가사는 / 거의 쓰러질듯했지만 무사한 /

was gathered into her mother's arms.
엄마의 품에 안겼다

Jimmy Valentine put on his coat, / and walked outside the
지미 발렌타인은 코트를 입고 / 난간 밖으로 걸어갔다 /

railings / towards the front door.
정문을 향하여

As he went / he thought / he heard / a far-away voice /
그가 갈 때 / 그는 생각했다 / 들었다고 / 희미한 목소리를 /

---

immovable 움직이지 않는 under a spell 마법에 걸린 pet 특히 좋아하는 bite (기계가) 베어 들다, 파고들다
burglarious 절도의 bolt 볼트 collapse 무너지다

that had called him "Ralph!"
(어떤 목소리일까?) 그를 "랠프!" 라고 부르는

He once knew / it / but he never hesitated.
예전에 알고 있었다 /   그 목소리를 / 그러나 그는 주저하지 않았다

At the door a big man / stood in his way.
문에는 덩치 큰 남자가 /   앞을 가로막았다

"Hello, Ben!" said Jimmy, / still with his strange smile.
안녕 벤!   지미가 말했다 /   여전히 이상한 미소를 띠며

"You're here at last, aren't you? Well, let's go.
마침내 나타나셨군요? 그렇지 않아요   자, 갑시다

I know that it makes no difference, / now."
그건 별로 중요한 일 같지 않아 / 이제는(it =사랑하는 여인 앞에서 금고털이 범으로 끌려가는 일)

And then Ben Price acted / rather strangely.
그러나 그때 벤 프라이스는 행동했다 /   좀 이상하게

"Guess you're mistaken, Mr. Spencer," he said.
뭔가 오해하신 것 같은데요, 스펜서씨   그가 말했다.

"Don't believe / I recognize you.
 생각하지 않아요 /   내가 선생님을 안다고(선생님은 모르는 분이라고 생각해요)

Your buggy's waiting for you, ain't it?"
당신의 마차가 기다리고 있소, 그렇지 않아요?

And Ben Price turned / and strolled down / the street.
그리고 벤 프라이스는 몸을 돌리고 /   걸어 내려갔다 /   거리를

> ### Key Expression
>
> #### ~인 것 같아요
> 1. guess(~인 것 같다); 잘 모르지만 추측하여 자신의 의견을 표현할 때 사용한다. "suppose"를 사용하면 비슷한 의미가 전달된다.
>   I guess that she is about 30. 잘 모르지만 그녀는 30세정도 인 것 같아요.
>   I suppose he is a novelist. 그는 소설가인 것 같아요.
> 2. believe(~라고 생각하다); 완전히 확신할 수 없지만, 어떤 일이 가능하거나 사실이라고 생각할 때, 사용한다.
>   I believe it will rain tomorrow. 내 생각엔 내일 비가 올 것 같아요.
> 3. feel; 사실이아니라 감정을 토대로 하여 자신의 의견을 표현할 때 사용한다.
>   I feel that there is no alternative. 다른 대안이 없는 것 같아요.
> 4. suspect; 뭔가 불쾌한 사건에 대해 자신의 의견을 표현할 때 사용한다.
>   I suspect that he told a lie. 그가 거짓말 한 것 같아요.

stand in one's way 길을 막다, 방해하다   make no difference 문제가 아니다, 차이가 없다
mistaken 오해한, 잘 못 생각하고 있는

Quiz 9

A. 내용 이해하기

다음 문장을 읽고 본문의 내용과 맞으면 T(True), 틀리면 F(False)를 쓰세요.

1. Annabel didn't recognize what Jimmy had done before he came to Elmore until he and Annabel were engaged to be married.
2. Jimmy wrote to his friend to sell his tool set at $ 1,000.
3. Jimmy opened the safe without using his tool set.
4. Ben Price didn't arrest Jimmy because he didn't have enough evidence.

B. 단어

다음 제시된 단어의 설명을 읽고, 어떤 단어의 정의를 설명하는지 아래의 박스에서 찾아 써 보세요.

1. to show respect and love for somebody
2. a close friend; chum
3. a series of numbers or letters you need to open a lock
4. to go somewhere even though it could be dangerous
5. a special quality someone has that makes people like them
6. extremely worried and frightened about a situation
7. to walk in a slow relaxed way; to stroll
8. to succeed in doing something after trying very hard; achieve
9. to move suddenly in a particular direction by jumping
10. to attract someone very much and hold their attention by charm or beauty
11. to make an exact copy of something
12. a feeling of liking or loving somebody and caring him
13. having an extremely good ability to see

---

accomplish captivate charm affection pal duplicate venture
saunter combination spring frantic worship keen

Answer A. 1. T 2. F 3. F 4. F

B. 1. worship 2. pal 3. combination 4. venture 5. charm 6. frantic 7. saunter 8. accomplish 9. spring 10. captivate 11. duplicate 12. affection 13. keen

C. 직독직해

아래에 제시된 문장을 직독직해로 해석해보세요.

1. He was as much at home / in the family of Mr. Adams / and that of Annabel's married sister / as if he were already a member.

   →

2. Annabel, / whose heart was bubbling / with happiness and lively youth, / put on Jimmy's hat, and picked up the suit-case.

   →

3. Suddenly there was a scream or two / from the women, / and a commotion.

   →

4. During the following silence / they could just hear / the faint sound of the child / wildly shrieking / in the dark vault / in a panic of terror.

   →

D. 동시통역

아래에 제시된 직독직해를 보고, 영어로 말해보세요.

1. 1년이 지났을 때 / 랠프 스펜서의 상황은 이랬다.

   →

2. 그는 어슬렁어슬렁 걸어 들어왔고 / 팔꿈치로 턱을 괴었다.

   →

3. 그는 단지 기다리고 있었다 / (누구를?) 그가 아는 사람을.

   →

4. 문에는 덩치 큰 남자가 / 앞을 가로막았다.

   →

Answer

C. 1. 그는 마음 편하게 지냈다 / 아담스씨의 집에서나 / 애너벨의 결혼한 언니의 집에서나 / 마치 그가 벌써 (가족의) 일원이 된 것처럼 2. 애너벨은 / 그녀의 마음은 흥분하고 있었던 / 행복과 발랄한 젊음으로 / 지미의 모자를 쓰고 여행 가방을 들어올렸다. 3. 갑자기 비명소리가 한두 번 들렸다 / 부인들 사이에서 / 그리고 큰 소동이 벌어졌다. 4. 계속 이어지는 침묵 동안에 / 그들은 겨우 들을 수 있었다 / 희미한 아이의 소리를 / (어떤 아이?) 마구 비명을 지르고 있었던 / 어두운 금고 속에서 / 공포 때문에 당황하여

D. 1. At the end of a year / the situation of Mr. Ralph Spencer was this. 2. He sauntered in / and leaned on his elbow. 3. He was just waiting / for a man he knew. 4. At the door a big man / stood in his way.

The Cop and the Anthem
경찰과 찬송가

SCENE 1

On his bench in Madison Square / Soapy moved uneasily.
메디슨 광장에 있는 벤치에서 / 소피는 걱정하며 몸을 움직였다

When wild geese begin to fly south, /
기러기가 남쪽으로 날아가기 시작할 때 /

and when women without sealskin coats /
그리고 물개가죽 코트가 없는 여인들이 /

grow kind to their husbands, /
남편에게 친절해질 때 /

and when Soapy moves uneasily / on his bench /
그리고 소피가 걱정하며 몸을 움직일 때 / 자신의 벤치에서 /

in the park, / you may know / that winter is near at hand.
공원에서 / 당신은 알 것이다 / 겨울이 가까이 왔음을

A dead leaf fell / in Soapy's lap.
낙엽 한 개가 떨어졌다 / 소피의 무릎에

That was Jack Frost's calling card.
그것은 잭 프로스트(서리)의 명함이었다

Jack is kind / to the inhabitants / of Madison Square, /
잭(서리)은 친절하다 / 살고 있는 사람들에게 / 메디슨 광장에서 /

and warns them / of his annual call.
그리고 그들에게 경고한다 / 그가 해마다 찾아온다는 것을

At the corners of four streets, / he hands his calling cards /
사거리의 모퉁이에서 / 그(서리)는 자신의 명함을 준다 /

to the North Wind, /
북풍에게 /

so that the inhabitants may make ready /
그러면 (메디슨 광장에) 살고 있는 사람들이 준비할 수 있다 /

for the coming winter.
다가오는 겨울에

inhabitant 거주자 warn 경고하다 annual 해마다의, 1년의 call (짧은) 방문

Soapy realized the fact / that the time had come /
소피는 그 사실을 알게 되었다 / (어떤 사실을?)시기가 왔다는 것을 /

for him to find ways /
그가 방법을 찾아야 하는 /

to provide against the coming winter.
다가오는 겨울에 준비하는

And therefore he moved uneasily / on his park bench.
그래서 그는 걱정스럽게 움직였다 / 공원 벤치에서

Soapy did not have very high hopes / for the winter.
소피는 대단한 희망이 있는 것이 아니었다 / 겨울을 (잘 지내려는)

In them there were no considerations /
그의 소망엔 생각하지도 않았다 /

of cruising on a ship / in the Mediterranean, /
배를 타고 유람하는 것을 / 지중해에서

of sailing away on a ship /
(생각하지도 않았다) 배를 타고 유람하는 /

in the Bay of Naples.
나폴리 만에서

Three months / in the prison on the Blackwell's Island /
3달 (동안 보내는 것)이 / 블랙웰 섬에 있는 감옥에서 /

was what he craved.
그가 갈망하는 것이었다

Three months of assured board and bed /
3달 동안 보장된 식사와 침대와 /

and congenial company, /
마음에 맞는 친구는 /

safe from the cold north wind
북풍과 경찰로부터 안전하면서 /

and cops, / seemed to Soapy /
소피에게는 보였다 /

the most desirable thing in the world.
세상에서 가장 매력적인 것처럼

For years / the prison on the Island /
수년 동안 / 블랙웰 섬에 있는 감옥은 /

had been his winter quarters.
소피의 겨울 주거지였다

While his more fortunate fellow New Yorkers had bought /
좀 더 운이 좋은 뉴욕 사람들이 구입하는 동안에 /

their tickets to Palm Beach / each winter, /
팜비치로 가는 표를 /   매년 겨울마다 /

Soapy had made his humble arrangements / to move /
소피는 소박하게 준비했다 /   이동하려고 /

into Blackwell Prison.
블랙웰 섬에 있는 감옥으로

Key Expression

grow+형용사; (차츰) ~이 되다, 되어가다

"grow" 동사는 "become"의 뜻으로 "get", 또는 "go" 동사와 같은 의미지만, 더 격식을 차린 표현이다.
The sound grew fainter. 그 소리는 더 약하게 들렸다.
She has grown tired of being an actress. 그녀는 싫증나게 되었다 / 배우인 것이
She grew more and more in love with him. 그녀는 더욱더 사랑하게 되었다 / 그를

provide against 준비하다, 대비하다 cruising 유람하는 것, 유람 bay 만 crave 갈망하다 board 식사
congenial 마음이 맞는
desirable 매력적인, 탐나는, 바람직한 quarter 주거지 arrangement 준비, 계획

SCENE 2

And now the time had come.
그리고 이제 때가 왔다

On the previous night / three Sunday newspapers, /
전날 밤에 / 일요일 신문 3개는 /

some beneath his coat, some over his lap, /
일부는 코트 밑에 넣고, 일부는 무릎 위에 덮었던 /

had failed to repulse the cold / as he slept on his bench /
추위를 내쫓는 데는 실패했다 / 그가 벤치 위에서 잤을 때 /

near the spurting fountain / in the ancient square.
(어디 있는 벤치?) 물을 뿜어대는 분수대 근처에 있던 / (어디 있는 분수대?) 오래된 광장에 있는

So the Island loomed / big and timely / in Soapy's mind.
그래서 그 섬(으로 이동하는 일)은 나타났다 / 중요하고 시기에 알맞은 것처럼 / 소피의 마음에

He scorned the provisions / made in the name of charity /
그는 시설을 비웃었다 / 자선이라는 이름으로 만들어진 /

for the city's dependents. In Soapy's opinion /
이 도시의 식객을 위해 소피의 의견으로는 /

the Law was more benign than Philanthropy.
법률이 박애보다 더 인자했다 (소피는 자선단체가 제공하는 식사, 숙박시설보다 감옥에서 생활하는 것이 더 좋다고 생각했다)

There were many charitable institutions, /
자선단체가 많았다 /

both municipal and religious, /
시나 종교단체가 운영하는 /

on which he might receive lodging and food /
이런 단체에서 그는 숙박과 음식을 받을 수도 있었다 /

accordant with the simple life.
소박한 생활에 맞는

But to Soapy's proud spirit /
그러나 소피처럼 자존심이 강한 사람에게 /

the gifts of charity are burdensome.
자선의 선물은 거추장스러운 것이었다

If not in coin / you must pay in humiliation of spirit /
돈이 아니더라도 / 영혼의 굴욕이라는 대가를 치러야 한다 /

for every benefit / received at the hands of philanthropy.
모든 혜택에 대해서 / 박애의 손길에 의해서 받는

Whenever he got something for free, / his pride was hurt.
그가 뭔가를 공짜로 받을 때마다 / 그의 자존심은 상처를 받았다

Every bed of charity / must have its toll of a bath, /
모든 자선의 침대에는 / 반드시 목욕이라는 희생이 있었고 /

(노숙자가 자선단체의 도움을 받아 공짜로 자려면, 그들이 악취가
나기 때문에 목욕을 해야 한다. 이런 과정은 소피에게 치욕스럽고
자존심에 상처를 준다.)

every loaf of bread / its price of a private and personal questions.
모든 빵 조각에는 / 사적이고 개인적인 질문을 받는 대가를 치러야 했다
(공짜로 음식을 먹으려면, 수많은 사적인 질문에 대답해야 했다)

So it is better to be a guest of the law, /
그래서 법률의 손님이 되는(감옥에 가는) 편이 더 낫다 /

which though conducted by rules, /
(법률이란) 비록 규칙에 의해 시행되지만 /

does not meddle unduly / with a gentleman's private affairs.
부당하게 참견하지는 않는다 / 신사의 사적인 일에

Soapy, / having decided to go to the Island, /
소피는 / 그 섬으로 가기로 결심했던 /

at once set about / accomplishing his desire.
즉시 시작했다 / 자신의 소망을 성취하는 일을

There were many easy ways / of doing this.
쉬운 방법이 많이 있다 / 이것을 하는 데는

The most pleasant / was to dine luxuriously /
가장 즐거운 방법은 / 사치스럽게 식사를 하는 것이다 /

at some expensive restaurant; / and then, after declaring /
비싼 식당에서 / 그러고 나서 선언한 다음에 /

that he could not pay, / be handed over /
음식값을 지불할 수 없다고 / 인계되는 것이다 /

quietly and without uproar / to a policeman.
조용히 소란을 피우지 않고 / 경찰에게

An accommodating judge / would do the rest.
친절한 판사가 / 나머지 일을 처리할 것이다

---

previous 앞의, 전의 repulse 내쫓다 spurting 뿜어대는 loom 갑자기 크게 나타나다 provision 설비, 시설
charity 자선 dependent 타인에게 의존하여 사는 사람, 식객 benign 인자한 philanthropy 박애
charitable 자선의 municipal 시의 lodging 숙박 accordant 일치하여, 조화하여
spirit (형용사와 함께) ~한 기질의 사람 proud spirit 자존심이 강한 사람 burdensome 거추장스러운
humiliation 굴욕 toll 희생 conduct 시행하다 meddle 참견하다 unduly 부당하게, 과도하게
set about 시작하다 dine 식사하다 uproar 소란 accommodating 친절한

SCENE 3

Soapy / who had decided what to do / left his bench /
소피는 /　　무엇을 해야 할지 결정했던 (소피는) /　　벤치에서 떠나 /

and strolled out of the square / and across the level sea of
광장에서 어슬렁어슬렁 걸어 나가서 /　　바다처럼 평평한 아스팔트를 건너갔다 /

asphalt, / where Broadway and Fifth Avenue flow together.
　　그곳에서 브로드웨이와 5번가가 만난다

Up Broadway he turned, / and halted at a glittering cafe, /
브로드웨이를 향하여 그는 돌아서 /　　(화려하게) 빛나고 있는 카페에서 멈췄다 /

where the choicest products of the grape are served,
그 카페에는 최고급 포도주가 나오고 /

and the best people in the best clothes / appear every night.
가장 좋은 옷을 빼입은 세련된 사람들이 /　　밤마다 모여든다

Soapy had confidence / in his appearance /
소피는 자신감이 있었다 /　　자신의 모습에 /

from the lowest button / of his vest upward.
맨 아래 단추부터 /　　(어떤 단추?) 조끼의 위쪽에는

His face was shaven, / and his coat was decent /
면도도 했고 /　　코트는 괜찮았고 /

and his neat black tie / had been presented to him /
말끔한 검은 넥타이는 /　　선물로 받은 것이다 /

by a lady missionary / on Thanksgiving Day.
전도하는 어떤 여인으로부터 /　　추수감사절에

If he could reach a table in the restaurant / unsuspected /
만일 그가 그 식당의 테이블에 갈수 있다면 /　　의심 받지 않고 /

success would be his.
성공은 그의 것일 것이다 (그는 성공할 수 있다)

The part of him / that would show above the table /
그의 부분(모습)은 /　　(어떤 부분) 테이블 위로 보이는 /

would raise no doubt / in the waiter's mind.
어떤 의심도 일으키지 않을 것이다 /　웨이터의 마음에

A roasted duck, / thought Soapy, / would be about the thing /
구운 오리 고기가 /　　소피는 생각했다 /　　적당할 것이라고 /

-with a bottle of wine, / and then Camembert,
포도주 한 병과 함께 /　　그리고 나서는 카망베르 치즈와

a cup of strong coffee and a cigar.
진한 커피 한잔 그리고 시가 한 개와 함께

One dollar for the cigar would be enough.
시가 값으로 1달러면 충분할 것이다

The total would not be so high /
모두 합친 음식 값은 많이 나오지는 않을 것이다 /

as to demand an act of revenge /
복수하려는 행동이 필요할 만큼 /

from the cafe management; / and yet the meat would leave /
카페 직원으로부터 /   그리고 고기는 (어떤 상태가) 되게 할 것이다 /

him filled and happy / for the journey to his winter refuge.
소피가 배를 채우고 만족하게 하는 상태로 / 겨울 피난처로 가는 여행에

But as Soapy set foot / inside the restaurant door /
그러나 소피가 발을 들여놓았을 때 /   그 식당의 문 안으로 /

the head waiter saw / his frayed trousers and ruined shoes.
수석 웨이터는 쳐다보았다 /   그의 닳아빠진 바지와 낡은 신발을

Strong hands of several waiters turned him about /
웨이터 몇 명의 힘센 손이 (식당으로 들어오던) 그를 돌렸고 /

and conveyed him / in silence and haste / to the sidewalk /
보냈다(밀어냈다) /   조용하고 신속하게 / 보도로 /

So he missed the chance / to have the roasted duck.
그래서 그는 기회를 놓쳤다 /   구운 오리를 먹을 수 있는

Key Expression

so ~ as to 동사원형; ~할 정도로(~할 만큼의) 매우 ~한(하게)

He was so kind as to drop me off at my house.
그는 매우 친절했다 / 내 집 앞에서 내려줄 정도로
He got up so early as to be in time for the first train.
그는 매우 일찍 일어났다 / 시간에 맞출 정도로 / 첫 기차의
I am not so senseless as to do such a thing.
나는 어리석지 않다 / 그런 일을 할 정도로

glitter 빛나다 choice 최고의, 고급의 missionary 선교사,전도자 unsuspected 의심받지 않은 Camembert 부드럽고 맛이 짙은 프랑스 치즈 revenge 복수 fray 헤어지다, 닳게 하다 frayed 닳아빠진 convey 나르다, 보내다

SCENE 4

Soapy turned off Broadway.
소피는 브로드웨이에서 옆길로 빠졌다

It seemed / that his route to the coveted island /
(아마도~인 것 같아 보였다) / 그가 갈망하는 섬으로 가는 길은 /

was not to be an epicurean one. He must think /
미식가가 되는 길은 아닌 것 (같아 보였다)   그는 생각해야만 한다 /

of some other way / of getting to his winter haven.
다른 길(방법)을 /   겨울철 안식처로 가는

At a corner of Sixth Avenue /
6번가의 코너에서 /

electric lights and cunningly displayed wares /
전깃불과 재치 있게 진열된 상품은 /

behind plate-glass / made a shop window conspicuous.
두꺼운 유리판 뒤에 있는 /   가게의 진열창이 눈에 띄게 했다

Soapy picked up a stone / and threw it through the glass.
소피는 돌멩이 하나를 주워서 /   그 유리창에 던졌다

People came running around the corner, /
사람들이 모퉁이 주위로 달려왔다 /

a policeman in the lead. Soapy stood still, /
경찰관 한 명이 앞장서고   소피는 가만히 서있었다 /

with his hands in his pockets, / and smiled /
주머니에 손을 넣고 /   그리고 웃었다 /

at the sight of the cop. "Where's the man / that done that?"
경찰관을 보고는   어디 있지 그 사람은 / (어떤 사람?) 그런 일을 했던(유리창을 깼던)

inquired the officer excitedly.
경찰관이 흥분해서 물었다

"Don't you figure out / that I might have had something to do
생각하지 않으시나요? /   제가 이 일과 관련이 있다고 /

with it?" / said Soapy, / not without sarcasm, but friendly, /
        소피가 말했다 / 비꼬는 투가 없지 않았지만 친근하게 (말했다) /

as one greets good fortune.
행운을 맞이하는 사람처럼

The policeman's mind refused to accept /
그 경찰관의 마음은 받아들이지 않았다 /

148　O. Henry's Short Stories

Soapy as a suspect. Men who smash windows /
소피를 혐의자로   유리를 깨는 인간들은 /

do not remain there / to talk to / cops.
그곳에 남아있지 않는다 / 이야기하려고 / 경찰관과

They take to their heels. The policeman saw / a man /
그들은 도망간다(라고 경찰은 생각했다) 그 경찰관은 봤다 / 한 남자가 /

half way down the block / running to catch a car.
반 블록쯤 아래에서 / 차를 잡으려고 뛰어가고 있는 것을

With drawn club / he joined in the pursuit.
곤봉을 뽑아들고 / 그 경찰관은 추적에 가담했다(그 남자를 쫓아갔다)

Soapy, sick at heart, / loafed along, / twice unsuccessful.
소피는 / 속이 상해서, / 빈둥빈둥 걸었다 / 두 번이나 실패하자

On the opposite side of the street / was another restaurant.
거리 반대편에 /   식당 하나가 있었다

It catered to customers /
그 식당은 손님들에게 식사를 제공했다 /

with large appetites / who were not rich.
식욕은 굉장하나 / 주머니 사정은 넉넉하지 않은 (손님에게)

Its plates and atmosphere were thick; /
그릇과 분위기는 두꺼웠다 /

its soup and tablecloths thin.
하지만 스프와 테이블보는 얇았다

Into this place Soapy took /
이 식당 안으로 소피는 가져갔다(들어갔다) /

his old shoes and torn trousers / without challenge.
낡은 신발과 찢어진 바지를 (입고) / 제지를 받지 않고

At a table he sat and consumed /
테이블에 그는 앉아서 먹었다 /

beefsteak, pancakes, doughnuts and pie.
비프스테이크, 팬케이크, 도넛과 파이를

And then to the waiter / he revealed the fact /
그러고 나서 웨이터에게 / 사실을 털어놓았다 /

that the minutest coin and himself were strangers.
(어떤 사실을?)작은 동전과 자신은 서로 모르는 사람이라는 것을(돈이 한 푼도 없다는 사실을)

---

covet 갈망하다 epicurean 미식가의 haven 안식처 ware 제품 plate-glass 판유리
conspicuous 눈에 잘 띄는 inquire 묻다 sarcasm 비꼼 suspect 혐의자 pursuit 추격
sick 속이 상해서, 짜증나서 cater 음식을 주다 without challenge 항의를 받지 않고, 제지를 받지 않고
consume ~을 먹다, 마시다 reveal (비밀을) 폭로하다, 밝히다 minute 아주 작은, 사소한

Quiz 10

A. 내용 이해하기

다음 문장을 읽고 본문의 내용과 맞으면 T(True), 틀리면 F(False)를 쓰세요.

1. Soapy's dream is to cruise on a ship in the Mediterranean.
2. Soapy doesn't like to be served by charitable organizations because they treated him badly.
3. Soapy failed to eat a roasted duck at the restaurant because of his shabby dress.
4. The policeman thought Soapy broke a window on purpose.

B. 단어

다음 제시된 단어의 설명을 읽고, 어떤 단어의 정의를 설명하는지 아래의 박스에서 찾아 써 보세요.

1. the practice of giving money to poor people and helping them
2. to want to have something very much that someone else has
3. to carry out a particular activity
4. pleasant to spend time with because it suits your character
5. to try to influence or change a situation without being asked
6. a place where people can live peacefully or stay safely
7. to tell someone about actual or potential harm in advance
8. one who lives in a particular place as a permanent resident
9. a situation in which people make a great deal of noise
10. a feeling of shame and great embarrassment
11. the number of people killed or injured in a particular disaster
12. the rooms that are given to someone to live
13. easy to notice; can be seen easily

> inhabitant warn congenial quarter philanthropy humiliation
> conspicuous toll conduct meddle uproar covet haven

Answer   A. 1. F 2. F 3. T 4. F
B. 1. philanthropy 2. covet 3. conduct 4. congenial 5. meddle 6. haven 7. warn 8. inhabitant 9. uproar
10. humiliation 11. toll 12. quarter 13. conspicuous

C. 직독직해

아래에 제시된 문장을 직독직해로 해석해보세요.

1. Three months of assured board and bed / and congenial company, / safe from the cold north wind and cops, / seemed to Soapy / the most desirable thing in the world.

    →

2. There were many charitable institutions, / both municipal and religious, / on which he might receive lodging and food / accordant with the simple life.

    →

3. The part of him / that would show above the table / would raise no doubt / in the waiter's mind.

    →

4. It seemed that his route to the coveted island / was not to be an epicurean one.

    →

D. 동시통역

아래에 제시된 직독직해를 보고, 영어로 말해보세요.

1. 당신은 알 것이다 / 겨울이 가까이 왔음을

    →

2. 그가 뭔가를 공짜로 받을 때마다 / 그의 자존심은 상처를 받았다.

    →

3. 그는 생각해야만 한다 / 다른 방법을 / 겨울철 안식처로 가는

    →

4. 그 경찰관의 마음은 받아들이지 않았다 / 소피를 혐의자로

    →

Answer

C. 1. 3달 동안 보장된 식사와 침대와 / 마음에 맞는 친구는 / 북풍과 경찰로부터 안전하면서 / 소피에게는 보였다 / 세상에서 가장 매력적인 것처럼 2. 자선단체가 많았다 / 시나 종교단체가 운영하는 / 이런 단체에서 그는 숙박과 음식을 받을 수도 있었다 / 소박한 생활에 맞는 3. 그의 부분(모습)은 / (어떤 부분) 테이블 위로 보이는 / 어떤 의심도 일으키지 않을 것이다 / 웨이터의 마음에 4. (아마도) 그가 갈망하는 섬으로 가는 길은 / 미식가가 되는 길은 아닌 것 (같았다)

D. 1. you may know / that winter is near at hand. 2. Whenever he got something for free, / his pride was hurt. 3. He must think / of some other way / of getting to his winter haven. 4. The policeman's mind refused to accept / Soapy as a suspect.

SCENE 5

"Now, get busy and call a cop," said Soapy.
이제 서둘러서 경찰을 부르세요.   소피가 말했다

"And don't keep a gentleman waiting."
그리고 신사를 기다리게 하지 마세요.

"No cop for you," said the waiter, /
당신에게는 경찰이 필요 없어, 웨이터가 말했다 /

with a voice like butter cakes /
(어떤 웨이터?) 버터케이크 같은 목소리로 /

and an eye like the cherry in a Manhattan cocktail.
그리고 맨해튼 칵테일에 있는 체리 같은 눈을 가진

"Hey, Con!"
이봐, 콘!

The two waiters pitched Soapy /
두 명의 웨이터가 소피를 내던졌다 /

upon his left ear on the callous pavement.
소피의 왼쪽 귀가 딱딱한 보도에 철썩 붙도록

He arose, / joint by joint, / as a carpenter's rule opens, /
그는 일어났다 /   관절을 하나씩 펴면서 /   목수의 자가 펼쳐지듯이 /

and beat the dust / from his clothes.
그리고 먼지를 털어냈다 /   옷에서

Arrest seemed but a rosy dream.
체포되는 일은 단지 장밋빛 꿈처럼 보였다

The Island seemed very far away.
그 섬은 굉장히 멀리 떨어져 있는 것처럼 보였다

A policeman / who stood before a drug store /
경찰관은 /   (어떤 경찰관?) 약국 앞에 서있던 /

two doors away / laughed and walked down the street.
(그 약국은 소피로부터) 집 두 채 정도의 간격으로 떨어져 있는 / 웃고는 거리를 걸어갔다

Five blocks Soapy travelled / before he gained the courage /
다섯 블록을 소피는 걸어갔다 /   용기를 내기 전에 /

to try again.
다시 (체포되려고) 시도하려는

This time the opportunity presented /
이번에는 기회가 왔다 /

what he described / as a "cinch."
(어떤 기회?) 그가 말할 수 있는 / 누워서 떡먹기라고

A nice-looking young woman was standing before a
예쁘고 젊은 여성이 / 가게 진열창 앞에 서있었다 /

show window / gazing with great interest /
　　　　　　　아주 관심 있게 바라보면서 /

at its display of shaving mugs and ink-stands, /
(무엇을 보고 있을까?) 면도용 컵과 잉크스탠드가 진열된 것을 /

and two yards from the window /
그리고 진열창에서 2야드 떨어진 곳에 /

a large policeman with severe expression /
덩치가 크고 엄격한 표정을 한 경찰관이 /

leaned against a water plug.
소화전에 기대어 서 있었다

It was Soapy's plan / to bother the young lady /
소피의 계획이었다 /　　　　젊은 여성을 괴롭혀서 /

and be arrested / on a charge of harassment.
체포되는 것이었다 /　　여성을 괴롭힌 혐의로

The combination /
결합되어 /

of the refined and elegant appearance of his victim /
세련되고 우아한 그의 희생자의 모습과 /

and the conscientious cop /
양심적인 경찰관이 /

encouraged him to believe /
그가 믿도록 용기를 주었다 / (무엇을 믿도록?)

that he would soon feel /
그는 곧 느끼게 될 것이라고 /

the pleasant cop's hand upon his arm /
기분 좋은 경찰관의 손이 그의 팔을 잡는 것을 /

that would insure his winter quarters / on the Island.
(그런 경찰의 손은) 그가 겨울을 보낼 수 있는 숙소를 보장해줄 / 작은 섬에서

---

pitch 던지다 callous 딱딱해진, 무감각한 rule 자, 척도 describe A as B A를 B라고 말하다
cinch 누워서 떡먹기, 아주 쉬운 일 gaze 바라보다, severe 엄격한 lean 기대다 harassment 괴롭히는 일, 학대
refined 세련된 elegant 우아한 conscientious 양심적인 encourage ~에게 ~하도록 용기를 주다
insure 보장하다 quarters 숙소, 숙박소

SCENE 6

Soapy straightened / the lady missionary's ready-made tie /
소피는 똑바르게 폈고 /   전도하는 여자가 준 기성품 넥타이를 /

and wore his hat / tilted to one side.
모자를 쓰고 있었다   한 쪽으로 기울게

And he walked / toward the young woman.
그리고 그는 걸어갔다 /   그 젊은 여자를 향해서

He made eyes at her, / cleared his throat loudly, /
그는 여자에게 추파를 던졌고 /   큰소리로 헛기침 소리를 냈고 /

smiled, smirked /
싱글벙글 웃고 능글맞게 웃었다

and made the offensive and ill-mannered remarks /
그리고 모욕적이고 무례한 말을 했다 /

of the "womanizer."
"플레이보이" 의

Out of the corner of his eye, / Soapy saw /
곁눈으로 /   소피는 봤다 /

that the policeman was watching him / fixedly.
경찰관이 자기를 지켜보고 있는 것을 /   물끄러미

The young woman moved away / a few steps, /
그 젊은 여자는 물러섰다 /   몇 발짝 /

and again kept looking / at the shaving mugs on display.
그리고 다시 쳐다보았다 /   진열되어 있는 면도용 컵을

Soapy, boldly stepping to her side, / raised his hat and said: /
소피는 대담하게 그녀 옆에 가면서 /   모자를 들어올리며 말했다 /

"Ah there, Bedelia!
아, 베델리아!

Don't you want to come and play / with me?"
놀지 않을래 /   나와 함께?

The policeman was still looking.
그 경찰관은 여전히 지켜보고 있었다

The persecuted young woman /
괴롭힘을 당하던 젊은 여자가 /

had only to beckon a finger / to call the cop over, /
손가락으로 신호를 보내기만 하면 /   경찰에게 소리쳐 오라고 /

and Soapy would be on his way / to his insular haven.
그러면 소피는 가기 시작할 것이다 / 섬의 피난처로

Already he imagined / he could feel /
이미 그는 상상했다 / 그가 느낄 수 있다고 /

the cozy warmth of the station-house.
경찰서의 아늑한 따스함을

The young woman faced him / and, stretching out a hand, /
그 젊은 여자는 소피를 마주보았고 / 손을 뻗치면서 /

caught Soapy's coat sleeve. "Sure, Mike," she said joyfully,
소피의 코트 소매를 잡았다 좋아, 마이크 그녀가 유쾌하게 말했다

"if you'll blow me / to a few drinks.
당신이 나에게 사준다면 / 술을

I would have spoken to you sooner, /
나는 진작 네게 말하고 싶었는데 /

but the cop was watching." With the young woman /
경찰이 보고 있었어 그 젊은 여자와 함께 /

holding his arm / as ivy clings to his oak /
그의 손을 잡고 있는 / 담쟁이가 떡갈나무에 붙어 있는 것처럼 /

Soapy walked past the policeman / overcome with gloom.
소피는 경찰의 앞을 지나갔다 / 우울한 기분 때문에 맥을 못 추고

He seemed doomed to liberty. At the next corner /
그는 자유롭게 살아야 할 운명인 것 같았다 다음 모퉁이에서 /

he shook off his companion / and ran.
그는 동행하던 여자를 뿌리치고 / 뛰어갔다

He halted in a district / where streets are lighter, /
그는 어느 지역에서 멈췄다 / (그곳은) 거리는 더 밝고 /

and people are more lively / at night.
사람들은 더 활기에 차있는 곳에서 / 밤이면

Women in furs and men in great coats / moved gaily /
모피를 입은 여자들과 근사한 코트를 입은 남자들이 / 유쾌하게 움직였다 /

in the wintry air.
겨울의 공기 속에서

---

straighten (넥타이를) 똑바르게 펴다 ready-made 기성품의 tilt 기울이다 make eyes at ~에게 추파를 던지다
clear one's throat 헛기침을 하다 smirk 능글맞게 웃다 offensive 무례한, 불쾌한
womanizer 플레이보이, 난봉꾼 watch fixedly 계속(물끄러미) 쳐다보다 persecute 괴롭히다
beckon ~을 손짓으로 부르다(신호하다) insular 섬의 haven 피난처, 은신처 cozy 아늑한 joyfully 유쾌하게
blow ~을 사다, ~에게 한턱내다 overcome 맥을 못 추게 하다, 무력화시키다 gloom 우울
liberty 해방, 석방, 자유 shake off 따돌리다 gaily 유쾌하게, 명랑하게

SCENE 7

A sudden fear seized / Soapy.
갑작스런 공포가 사로잡았다 / 소피를

He wondered / if some dreadful enchantment had made /
그는 생각했다 / 어떤 무서운 마법이 하게했다고 /

him immune to arrest.
그가 체포되지 않도록

The thought brought / him a little of panic.
그런 생각은 가져왔다 / 그에게 약간의 두려움을(그런 생각을 하자 그는 조금 겁이 났다)

When he came upon another policeman /
그가 또 다른 경찰을 만났을 때 /

lounging grandly / in front of a luminous theater /
당당하게 어슬렁거리고 있던 / 밝게 빛나는 극장 앞에서 /

he caught / at the straw of "disorderly conduct."
그는 매달렸다 / '무질서한 행동' 이라는 지푸라기에

On the sidewalk, / Soapy began to yell /
보도 위에서 / 소피는 외치기 시작했다 /

drunken gibberish / at the top of his voice.
주정뱅이처럼 횡설수설하며 / 목청껏

He danced, howled, raved / and disturbed the passers-by.
그는 춤췄고 부르짖고 고함쳤다 / 그리고 지나가는 행인들을 방해했다

The policeman twirled his club, / turned his back to Soapy /
그 경찰은 곤봉을 빙빙 돌리면서 / 소피에게 등을 돌리고 /

and remarked to a citizen.
한 시민에게 말했다

"He must be one of those Yale boys /
그는 예일 대학생일 것입니다 /

celebrating their victory / over Hartford College in football.
승리를 축하하는 / 하트포드 대학을 축구 경기에서 이겨서

Noisy; but no harm.
시끄럽지만 해를 끼치진 않죠

We've instructions / to leave them shout."
지시를 받았어요 / 그들이 소리치도록 내버려 두라고

Hopelessly, Soapy ceased / his unavailing racket.
어쩔 수 없이 소피는 중지했다 / 효과 없는 소란을

O. Henry's Short Stories

Would never a policeman lay hands on him?
경찰이 그를 체포하지 않을까?

In his fancy / the Island seemed an unattainable paradise.
그의 환상 속에서 / 섬은 도달할 수 없는 이상향처럼 보였다

He buttoned his thin coat / against the chilling wind.
그는 얇은 코트의 단추를 채웠다 / 싸늘한 바람을 막으려고

In a cigar store he saw / a well-dressed man /
시가 가게에서 그는 봤다 / 잘 차려 입은 남자를 /

lighting a cigar. His silk umbrella he had set /
시가에 불을 붙이고 있는 비단 우산을 그는 놓았다 /

by the door / on entering. Soapy stepped inside, /
문간에 / 들어올 때 소피는 안으로 들어가서 /

took the umbrella / and sauntered off / with it slowly.
우산을 집어 들고 / 어슬렁어슬렁 걸어 나왔다 / 우산을 가지고 천천히

The well-dressed man followed him / quickly.
잘 차려입은 남자는 그를 쫓아왔다 / 급하게

"My umbrella," he said, sternly.
내 우산이요 그가 엄하게 말했다

"Oh, is it?" sneered Soapy, /
아, 그래요? 소피는 비웃었다 /

adding insult to petit larceny.
좀도둑질에다가 모욕까지 더하면서 (그의 물건을 훔치고 모욕까지 하면서)

"Well, why don't you call a policeman? I took it.
그럼 경찰을 부르지 그래요? 내가 우산을 훔쳤다고

Your umbrella! Why don't you call a cop?
당신 우산이요! 경찰을 부르지 그래요?

There stands one / on the corner."
경찰 한 명이 서 있군 / 저기 모퉁이에

The umbrella owner slowed his steps.
그 우산 주인은 걸음을 늦추었다

Soapy did likewise, / with a presentiment
소피도 또한 그랬다 (걸음을 늦추었다) / 예감하면서 /

that luck would again run against him.
행운이 다시 달아나버릴 것이라는

seize 사로잡다 wonder ~이 아닐까라고 생각하다 enchantment 마법 immune ~을 당할 염려가 없는 lounge 어슬렁거리다 luminous 빛나는 disorderly 무질서한 gibberish 횡설수설 howl 부르짖다, 큰 소리로 외치다 rave 고함치다 twirl 빙빙 돌리다 remark 말하다 instruction 지시 cease 중지하다 unavailing 효과 없는 racket 소음, 법석 unattainable 도달하기 어려운 saunter 어슬렁어슬렁 걷다 sneer 비웃다 insult 모욕 petit 작은 사소한 larceny 도둑질 petit larceny 좀도둑질 likewise 역시, 또 presentiment 예감

The policeman looked at the two / curiously.
그 경찰관은 두 남자를 바라보았다 / 호기심을 가지고

"Of course," said the umbrella man, /
"물론" 그 우산 주인이 말했다 /

"that is-well, you know how these mistakes occur.
말하자면 저어, 왜 이런 실수는 흔히 일어나는 법이죠

If it's your umbrella, / I hope / you'll excuse me.
이것이 당신 우산이라면 / 바래요 / 저를 용서해주시길

I picked it up / this morning in a restaurant.
이것을 주웠어요 / 오늘 아침에 어느 식당에서

If you recognize it as yours, / I hope you'll-"
당신 것이라고 알아본다면 / 저는 당신이..."

"Of course it's mine," said Soapy, viciously.
"물론 제 것이죠" 소피가 심술궂게 말했다.

Key Expression

직독직해를 잘 하려면, 상황에 맞게 숙어의 의미를 연상해야 한다.

"shake off"도 상황에 따라 의미가 다르다.

1. shake off; (뒤쫓는 사람을) 따돌리다

   He shook off the police.
   그는 뒤쫓는 경찰을 따돌렸다
   He shook off the car that was following him.
   그는 따돌렸다 / 자동차를 / 그를 뒤쫓던

2. shake off; 없애다

   I can't shake off this cold.
   감기를 떨쳐버릴 수 없어.
   He shook off his image as a pushy boss.
   그는 이미지를 떨쳐버렸다 / 주제넘게 간섭하는 관리자라는

recognize ~으로 알다, 인정하다 viciously 심술궂게

SCENE 8

The ex-umbrella man retreated.
우산의 전 주인은 물러섰다

The policeman hurried to assist /
그 경찰관은 도와주려고 바쁘게 갔다 /

a tall blonde in a long coat /
긴 코트를 입은 키 큰 금발여자를 /

across the street in front of a street car /
전차의 앞에 있는 거리를 건너서 /

that was approaching two blocks away.
(그 전차는) 두 블록 떨어진 곳에서 다가오고 있었던

Soapy walked eastward / through a street under
소피는 동쪽으로 걸어갔다 /   도로 공사 중인 거리를 지나서

construction.

He hurled the umbrella / wrathfully / into an open hole.
그는 그 우산을 세게 던졌다 /   격분하여 /   구덩이에

He muttered against the men /
사람들에게 마구 투덜댔다 /

who wear helmets and carry clubs.
(어떤 사람들?) 헬멧을 쓰고 경찰 봉을 들고 있는

Because he wanted to / fall into their hands, /
그는 바랐는데 /   체포되기를 /

they seemed to regard / him as a king /
그들은 생각했던 것 같았기 때문이다 / 소피를 왕처럼 /

who could do no wrong.
(그 왕은?) 어떤 과오도 저지를 리가 없는

At length Soapy reached / one of the avenues to the east /
마침내 소피는 도착했다 /   동쪽의 큰 길 중 한 곳에

where lights shone faintly / and it was far quieter.
그곳에는 가로등이 희미하게 빛났고 /   훨씬 더 조용했다

---

retreat 물러서다 wrathfully 격분하여 mutter 투덜대다 regard 생각하다, 간주하다
could do no wrong 과오를 저지를 리가 없다

He walked south toward Madison Square, /
그는 매디슨 광장을 향해 남쪽으로 걸었다 /

for the homing instinct survived /
왜냐하면 집으로 돌아가고 싶은 본능은 살아있었기 때문이다 /

even though the home was a park bench.
비록 집이 공원 벤치일지라도

But on an unusually quiet corner /
그러나 이상하리만치 조용한 모퉁이에서 /

Soapy came to a standstill.
소피는 멈췄다

Here was an old church, / quaint and gabled.
거기에는 오래된 교회가 하나 있었다 / (어떤 교회?) 진귀하고 박공이 있는

Through one violet-stained window / a soft light glowed, /
보라색으로 착색된 유리를 통해서 / 부드러운 빛이 반짝였다 /

where, no doubt, an organist / was making soft music /
그곳에서 틀림없이 오르간 주자가 / 부드러운 음악을 연주하고 있었다 /

to practice for the coming Sunday anthem.
다음 일요일의 찬송가를 연습하기위하여

Sweet music came / to Soapy's ears.
감미로운 음악이 흘러들어왔다 / 소피의 귀로

It caught him / transfixed / against the iron fence.
음악은 그를 사로잡았다 / 움직이지 못하도록 / 철책 담장 앞에서

The moon was above, lustrous and serene; /
달이 떠서 빛났고 구름한점 없었다 /

vehicles and pedestrians were few; /
차량과 행인들은 거의 없었다 /

sparrows twittered sleepily / in the eaves /
참새들이 졸린 듯이 짹짹거렸다 / 처마 끝에서 /

-for a little / while the scene /
아주 잠시 동안 / 한편 주위의 풍경이 /

might have been a country churchyard.
시골 교회의 마당 같았다

And the anthem / that the organist played /
그리고 찬송가는 / (어떤 찬송가?) 오르간 주자가 연주했던 /

cemented Soapy / to the iron fence, /
소피를 고정시켰다 / 철책 담장에 /

for he had known it well / in the younger days.
왜냐하면 그는 그것을 잘 알고 있었다 / 젊은 시절에

In those days his life contained /
그 시절에는 그의 생활속에 있었다 /

such things as mothers and roses and ambitions and
어머니와 장미와 야망과

friends and immaculate thoughts and collars.
친구와 깨끗한 생각과 옷깃 같은 것들이

The conjunction / of Soapy's receptive state of mind /
결합된 사건은(결합되어) / 뭔가를 순순히 받아들이려는 소피의 마음의 상태와 /

and the influences about the old church /
오래된 교회의 영향이 /

made a sudden and wonderful change / in his soul.
갑작스럽고 굉장한 변화를 만들었다 / 그의 영혼에

To his horror, / he saw the bottomless pit of the hell /
오싹하게도 / 그는 끝없는 지옥의 구덩이를 봤다 /

into which he had tumbled.
(그 구덩이 속으로) 그가 굴러 떨어졌던

He realized / that his life was full /
그는 깨달았다 / 그의 삶은 가득 차 있었다는 것을 /

of the degraded days, unworthy desires, dead hopes,
(무엇으로?) 타락한 시절, 천한 욕망, 죽은 희망들,

wrecked faculties and base motives.
못쓰게 된 재능과 천한 동기로

Key Expression

긴 명사구는 문장과 비슷하다?

The conjunction of Soapy's receptive state of mind / and the influences about the old church /
결합된 사건은(결합되어) / 뭔가를 받아들이려는 소피의 마음의 상태와 / 오래된 교회의 영향이 /

*"the conjunction of A and B"는 "A(state of mind)와 B(influences)가 결합된 사건(결합되어)"라는 의미다. "conjunction"대신 "combination"을 사용해도 된다.

*receptive state of mind; 타인의 의견이나 제안을 기꺼이 받아들이려는 마음의 상태

made a sudden and wonderful change / in his soul.
갑작스럽고 굉장한 변화를 만들었다 / 그의 영혼에

---

standstill 정지 quaint 진귀한 gabled 박공이 있는 violet-stained 보라색으로 착색된 anthem 찬송가 transfix ~을 고정시키다, 꼼짝 못하게 하다 lustrous 번쩍번쩍하는 serene 구름한점 없는, 맑은 pedestrian 행인 twitter 지저귀듯 지껄이다 eaves 처마, 차양 immaculate 결점 없는, 깨끗한 conjunction 결합 receptive (새로운 제안, 의견을) 쉽게 받아들이려는 tumble 구르다 tumble into (~안으로) 굴러 떨어지다 degrade 타락하다 wrecked 못쓰게 된 base 천한 motive 동기

SCENE 9

And also in a moment / his heart responded thrillingly /
그리고 또한 곧바로 /   그의 마음은 흥분해서 반응했다 /

to this novel mood.
이 새로운 분위기에

An instantaneous and strong impulse / moved him /
즉각적이고 강력한 충동이 /   그를 감동시켰다 /

to battle with his desperate fate.
자신의 절망적인 운명과 싸우도록

He would pull himself out / of the mire; /
그는 자신을 끌어낼 것이다 /   늪지(타락)에서 /

he would make a man of himself again; /
그는 다시 참된 자신을 되찾을 것이다 /

he would conquer the evil /
그는 악을 정복할 것이다 /

that had taken possession of him.
(그 악은) 자신을 사로잡았던

There was time. He was comparatively young yet.
시간이 있다   아직은 비교적 젊었다

He would resurrect / his old eager ambitions /
그는 부활시킬 것이다 /   지난날의 열렬한 야망을 /

and pursue them / without faltering.
추구할 것이다 /   망설이지 않고

Those solemn but sweet organ notes /
이 엄숙하지만 감미로운 오르간의 선율은 /

had set up a revolution in him.
그에게 획기적인 변화를 일으켰다

Tomorrow he would go into the roaring downtown district /
내일 그는 활기에 넘치는 번화가로 가서 /

and find work.
일자리를 찾을 것이다

A fur importer had once offered him / a place as a driver.
모피 수입상이 예전에 제의했던 적이 있었다 /   운전사 자리를

He would find him tomorrow / and ask for the position.
내일 그 사람을 만나서 /   자리를 부탁할 것이다

He would be somebody in the world. He would...
그는 세상에서 가치 있는 사람이 될 것이다   그도...

Soapy felt / a hand laid on his arm.
소피는 느꼈다 /   그의 팔에 손이 놓이는 것을

He looked quickly around / into the face of a policeman.
그가 얼른 돌아보았다 /   경찰관의 얼굴을

"What are you doing here?" asked the officer.
여기서 뭘 하고 있죠?   경찰관이 물었다

"Nothing," said Soapy.
아무 것도 안하고 있는데요, 소피가 말했다

"Then come along," said the policeman.
그러면 따라오시오   경찰관이 말했다

"Three months on the Island," said the judge /
섬에서 (징역) 3개월   판사가 말했다 /

in the Police Court / the next morning.
(경범죄를 처리하는) 즉결 재판소에서 / 다음날 아침

---

thrillingly 전율하며, 흥분하여 novel 새로운 instantaneous 즉각적인 impulse 충동 move 감동시키다
desperate 절망적인 mire 늪지 take possession of 사로잡다 comparatively 비교적 resurrect 부활시키다
pursue 추구하다, 쫓다 falter 망설이다 solemn 엄숙한, 장엄한 note 선율 roaring 활기에 넘치는, 활발한
importer 수입상 offer 제공하다, 주다 somebody 가치 있는 사람, 대단한 사람
Police Court 경찰 법원(경범죄를 즉결 재판하는 곳)

Quiz 11

A. 내용 이해하기

다음 문장을 읽고 본문의 내용과 맞으면 T(True), 틀리면 F(False)를 쓰세요.

1. Soapy was arrested by a policeman for trying to eat without paying money.
2. Soapy tried to seduce a young lady for pleasure.
3. Soapy didn't succeed in getting the umbrella.
4. At the church Soapy decided to get a job.

B. 단어

다음 제시된 단어의 설명을 읽고, 어떤 단어의 정의를 설명하는지 아래의 박스에서 찾아 써 보세요.

1. to bring back to life; to bring back into use
2. to stop doing something or stop something happening
3. a change caused by magic or the state of being under a magic spell
4. to smile in a silly or unpleasant manner
5. something that is very easy; a sure thing
6. not having good moral principles or rules
7. to give somebody a signal with your hand
8. very clean and tidy; free from stain
9. to complain about something, but without saying openly what you think
10. to treat someone cruelly or unfairly
11. different from anything known before; strikingly new
12. to make a lot of light chirping sounds
13. comfortable and friendly

> cinch smirk persecute beckon cozy enchantment cease mutter
> twitter immaculate base novel resurrect

A. 1. F 2. F 3. F 4. T
B. 1. resurrect 2. cease 3. enchantment 4. smirk 5. cinch 6. base 7. beckon 8. immaculate 9. mutter
10. persecute 11. novel 12. twitter 13. cozy

C. 직독직해

아래에 제시된 문장을 직독직해로 해석해보세요.

1. He arose, / joint by joint, / as a carpenter's rule opens, / and beat the dust / from his clothes.

    →

2. Soapy straightened / the lady missionary's ready-made tie / and wore his hat / tilted to one side.

    →

3. The policeman hurried to assist / a tall blonde in a long coat / across the street in front of a street car / that was approaching two blocks away.

    →

4. He walked south toward Madison Square, / for the homing instinct survived / even though the home was a park bench.

    →

D. 동시통역

아래에 제시된 직독직해를 보고, 영어로 말해보세요.

1. 소피는 경찰의 앞을 지나갔다 / 우울해져서

    →

2. 지시를 받았어요 / 그들이 소리치도록 내버려 두라고

    →

3. 이것이 당신 우산이라면 / 바래요 / 저를 용서해주시길

    →

4. 소피는 느꼈다 / 손이 놓이는 것을 / 그의 팔에

    →

Answer

C. 1. 그는 일어났다 / 관절을 하나씩 펴면서 / 목수의 자가 펼쳐지듯이 / 그리고 먼지를 털어냈다 / 옷에서 2. 소피는 똑바르게 폈고 / 전도하는 여자가 준 기성품 넥타이를 / 모자를 쓰고 있었다. / 한 쪽으로 기울게 3. 그 경찰관은 도와주려고 바쁘게 갔다 / 긴 코트를 입은 키 큰 금발여자를 / 전차의 앞에 있는 거리를 건너서 / (그 전차는) 두 블록 떨어진 곳에서 다가오고 있었던 4. 그는 매디슨 광장을 향해 남쪽으로 걸었다 / 집으로 돌아가고 싶은 본능은 살아있었기 때문이다 / 집이 공원 벤치일지라도

D. 1. Soapy walked past the policeman / overcome with gloom. 2. We've instructions / to leave them shout. 3. If it's your umbrella, / I hope / you'll excuse me. 4. Soapy felt / a hand laid on his arm.

O. Henry's Short Stories를 다시 읽어 보세요.

🍂 THE LAST LEAF 🍂

SCENE 1

In a little district west of Washington Square the streets have run crazy and broken themselves into small strips called "places." These "places" make strange angles and curves. One street crosses itself a time or two. An artist once discovered a valuable possibility in this street.

Suppose a collector with a bill for paints, paper and canvas should, in walking down this street, suddenly meet himself coming back, without receiving a cent!

So, to quaint old Greenwich Village the art people soon came prowling, hunting for north windows and eighteenth-century gables and Dutch attics and low rents.

Then they imported some pewter mugs and a chafing dish or two from Sixth avenue, and became a "colony." At the top of a squatty, three-story building Sue and Johnsy had their studio. "Johnsy" was familiar for Joanna.

One of the two young women was from Maine ; the other from California. They had met at a restaurant of Eighth street called "Delmonico's," and found their tastes in art, food, and clothes so congenial that the joint studio resulted.

SCENE 2

That was in May.

In November a cold, unseen stranger, whom the doctors called Pneumonia, stalked about the colony, touching one here and there with his icy fingers.

Over on the east side this ravager strode boldly, attacking his victims by scores, but his feet trod slowly through the maze of the narrow and moss-grown "places." Mr. Pneumonia was not what you would call a chivalric old gentleman.

A little woman from California was hardly fair game for the red-fisted, short-breathed old gentleman?

But Johnsy he smote; and she lay, scarcely moving, on her painted iron bedstead, looking through the small Dutch window-panes at the blank wall of the next brick house.

One morning the busy doctor invited Sue into the hallway with a shaggy, gray eyebrow.

"She has very small chance," he said, as he shook down the mercury in his clinical thermometer.

SCENE 3

"And that chance is for her to want to live.

Sometimes when people have waited for the undertaker, it doesn't matter what prescriptions I give. Your little lady has made up her mind that she's not going to get well. Has she anything on her mind?"

"She -she wanted to paint the Bay of Naples some day," said Sue.
"Paint? -bosh!

Has she anything on her mind worth thinking about twice -a man for instance?"

"A man?" said Sue, with a jew's twang in her voice.

"Is a man worth -but, no, doctor; there is nothing of the kind."
"Well, it is the weakness, then," said the doctor.

"I will do all that science can accomplish as much as possible. But whenever my patient begins to count the carriages in her funeral procession I subtract 50 percent from the curative power of medicines.

If you will get her to ask one question about the new winter styles in cloak sleeves, I will promise you a one-in-five chance for her, instead of one in ten."

SCENE 4

After the doctor had gone Sue went into the workroom and cried a Japanese napkin to a pulp. Then she swaggered into Johnsy's room with her drawing board, whistling ragtime. Johnsy lay, scarcely making a ripple under the bedclothes, with her face toward the window.

Sue stopped whistling, thinking she was asleep. She arranged her board and began a pen-and-ink drawing to illustrate a magazine story.

Young artists must pave their way to Art by drawing pictures for magazine stories that young authors write to pave their way to Literature.

As Sue was sketching a pair of elegant horseshow riding trousers and a monocle on the figure of the hero, an Idaho cowboy, she heard a low sound, several times repeated.

She went quickly to the bedside. Johnsy's eyes were open wide. She was looking out the window and counting, counting backward. "Twelve," she said, and a little later "eleven;" and then "ten," and "nine;" and then "eight" and "seven," almost together.

Sue looked anxiously out of the window. What was there to count? There was only a bare, dreary yard to be seen, and the blank wall of the brick house twenty feet away. An old, old ivy vine, gnarled and decayed at the roots, climbed half way up the brick wall.

SCENE 5

The cold breath of autumn had stricken its leaves from the vine until its skeleton branches clung, almost bare, to the bricks.

"What is it, dear?" asked Sue.

"Six," said Johnsy, in almost a whisper.

"They're falling faster now.

Three days ago there were almost a hundred.

It hurt my head to count them.

But now it's easy.

There goes another one.

There are only five left now."

"Five what, dear? Tell your Sue."

"Leaves. On the ivy vine.

When the last one falls I must go, too.

I've known that for three days.

Didn't the doctor tell you?"

"Oh, I never heard of such nonsense," complained Sue, with scorn.

"What have old ivy leaves to do with your getting well?

And you used to love that vine, you naughty girl.

Don't be a little fool."

SCENE 6

"Why, the doctor told me this morning that your chances for getting well real soon were -let's see exactly what he said -he said the chances were ten to one! Why, that's almost as good a chance as we have in New York when we ride on the street cars or walk past a new building. Try to take some broth now, and let Sudie go back to her drawing, so she can sell the editor man with it, and buy port wine for her sick child, and pork chops for her greedy self."

"You needn't get any more wine," said Johnsy, keeping her eyes fixed out the window.

"There goes another.

No, I don't want any broth.

That leaves just four.

I want to see the last one fall before it gets dark.

Then I'll go, too."

"Johnsy, dear," said Sue, bending over her, "will you promise me to keep your eyes closed, and not look out the window until I am done working?

I must hand those drawings in by tomorrow.

I need the light, or I would draw the shade down."

"Couldn't you draw in the other room?" asked Johnsy, coldly.

"I'd rather be here by you," said Sue.

"Besides I don't want you to keep looking at those silly ivy leaves."

SCENE 7

"Tell me as soon as you have finished," said Johnsy, closing her eyes, and lying white and still as a fallen statue, "because I want to see the last one fall.

I'm tired of waiting.

I'm tired of thinking.

I want to turn loose my hold on everything, and go sailing down, down, just like one of those poor, tired leaves."

"Try to sleep," said Sue.

"I must call Behrman up to be my model for the old hermit miner. I'll not be gone a minute.

Don't try to move till I come back."

Old Behrman was a painter who lived on the ground floor beneath them. He was past sixty and had a Michael Angelo's Moses beard curling down. Behrman was a failure in art. Forty years he had wielded the brush without getting near enough to touch the hem of his Mistress's robe. He had been always about to paint a masterpiece, but had never yet begun it. For several years he had painted nothing except now and then a daub in the line of commerce or advertising. He earned a little by serving as a model to those young artists in the colony who could not pay the price of a professional.

SCENE 8

He drank gin to excess, and still talked of his coming masterpiece. Also he was a fierce little old man, who scoffed terribly at softness in any one, and who regarded himself as a special guardian to protect the two young artists in the studio above.

Sue found Behrman smelling strongly of liquor in his dimly lighted den below.

In one corner was a blank canvas on an easel hat had been waiting there for twenty-five years to receive the first line of the masterpiece.

She told him of Johnsy's fancy, and how she feared she, light and fragile as a leaf herself, would float away when her slight hold upon the world grew weaker.

Old Behrman, with his red eyes streaming, shouted his contempt and derision for such idiotic imaginings.

"What!" he cried.

"Are there such fools? Do people die because leaves drop off from a damn vine?

I have not heard of such a thing.

No, I will not pose as a model for your dunderhead.

Why do you allow that silly Johnsy to think in such a thing? That poor little Miss Johnsy."

SCENE 9

"She is very ill and weak," said Sue, "and the fever has left her mind morbid and full of strange fancies.
Very well, Mr. Behrman, if you do not care to pose for me, you needn't. But I think you are a horrid old -talkative person."
"You are just like a woman!" yelled Behrman.
"Who said I will not pose as a model?
Go. I will come with you.
For half an hour I have been trying to say that I am ready to pose. God! This is not any place in which someone so good as Miss Johnsy lies sick. Some day I will paint a masterpiece, and we shall all go away.
God! yes."
Johnsy was sleeping when they went upstairs. Sue pulled the shade down to the window-sill, and motioned Behrman into the other room. In there they peered out the window fearfully at the ivy vine. Then they looked at each other for a moment without speaking. A persistent, cold rain was falling, mingled with snow.
Behrman, in his old blue shirt, took his seat as the hermit-miner on an upturned kettle for a rock.
When Sue awoke from an hour's sleep the next morning she found Johnsy with wide-open eyes staring at the drawn green shade.
"Pull it up; I want to see," she ordered, in a whisper.
Wearily Sue obeyed.

SCENE 10

But, lo! after the beating rain and fierce gusts of wind that had endured through the whole night, there yet stood out against the brick wall one ivy leaf. It was the last on the vine.

It was still dark green near its stem.

But at the edges it was tinted yellow with age and decay.

It hung bravely from a branch some twenty feet above the ground.

"It is the last one," said Johnsy.

"I thought it would surely fall during the night.

I heard the wind.

It will fall today, and I shall die at the same time."

"Dear, dear!" said Sue, leaning her worn face down to the pillow, "think of me, if you won't think of yourself. What would I do?"

But Johnsy did not answer. The most lonely thing in all the world is a soul when it is making ready to go on its mysterious, far journey. The fancy seemed to possess her more strongly as one by one the ties that bound her to friendship and to earth were loosed.

The day wore away, and even through the twilight they could see the lone ivy leaf clinging to its stem against the wall.

And then, with the coming of the night the north wind began to blow, while the rain still beat against the windows and pattered down from the low Dutch eaves.

SCENE 11

When it was light enough Johnsy again commanded that the shade be raised. The ivy leaf was still there. Johnsy lay for a long time looking at it. And then she called to Sue, who was stirring her chicken broth over the gas stove.

"I've been a bad girl, Sudie," said Johnsy.

"Something has made that last leaf stay there to show me how wicked I was. It is a sin to want to die. You may bring me a little broth now, and some milk with a little port in it, and -no; bring me a hand-mirror first, and then pack some pillows about me, and I will sit up and watch you cook."

An hour later she said. "Sudie, some day I hope to paint the Bay of Naples."

The doctor came in the afternoon, and Sue had an excuse to go into the hallway as he left.

"Even chances," said the doctor, taking Sue's thin, shaking hand in his. "With good nursing you'll win. And now I must see another case I have downstairs. Behrman, his name is -some kind of an artist, I believe. Pneumonia, too. He is an old, weak man, and the attack of Pneumonia is acute. There is no hope for him; but he goes to the hospital today to be made more comfortable."

SCENE 12

The next day the doctor said to Sue: "She's out of danger. You've won. Nutrition and care now -that's all."

And that afternoon Sue came to the bed where Johnsy lay, contentedly knitting a very blue and very useless woolen shoulder scarf, and put one arm around her, pillows and all.

"I have something to tell you, white mouse," she said.

"Mr. Behrman died of pneumonia today in the hospital.

He was ill only two days.

The janitor found him on the morning of the first day in his room downstairs helpless with pain. His shoes and clothing were wet through and icy cold. They couldn't imagine where he had been on such a dreadful night.

And then they found a lantern, still lighted, and a ladder that had been dragged from its place, and some scattered brushes, and a palette with green and yellow colors mixed on it, and looked out the window at the last ivy leaf on the wall.

Didn't you wonder why it never fluttered or moved when the wind blew?

Ah, darling, it's Behrman's masterpiece -he painted it there the night that the last leaf fell."

🍃 After Twenty Years 🍃

SCENE 1

The policeman on the beat moved up the avenue impressively. The impressiveness was habitual and not for show, for spectators were few.

The time was barely 10 o'clock at night, but chilly gusts of wind with a little rain had almost depeopled the streets.

Trying doors as he went, twirling his club with many intricate and artful movements, turning now and then to cast his watchful eye down the pacific thoroughfare, the officer, with his stalwart form and slight swagger, made a fine picture of a guardian of the peace. People in this part of the city kept early hours. Now and then you might see the lights of a cigar store or of an all-night lunch counter; but the majority of the doors belonged to business places that had been closed hours ago.

When about midway of a certain block the policeman suddenly slowed his walk.

In the doorway of a darkened hardware store a man leaned, with an unlighted cigar in his mouth.

As the policeman walked up to him the man spoke up quickly.

"It's all right, officer," he said, reassuringly.

"I'm just waiting for a friend.

It's an appointment made twenty years ago."

SCENE 2

"Sounds a little funny to you, doesn't it?", said the man.

"Well, I'll explain if you'd like to make certain it's all straight.

About that long ago there used to be a restaurant where this store stands.

'Big Joe' Brady's restaurant."

"Until five years ago," said the policeman.

"It was torn down then."

The man in the doorway struck a match and lit his cigar. The light showed a pale, square-jawed face with keen eyes, and a little white scar near his right eyebrow. His scarfpin was a large diamond, oddly set.

"Twenty years ago tonight," said the man, "I dined here at 'Big Joe' Brady's with Jimmy Wells, my best chum, and the finest chap in the world. He and I grew up together here in New York, just like two brothers. I was eighteen and Jimmy was twenty. The next morning I was to start for the West to make my fortune. You couldn't have dragged Jimmy out of New York; he thought it was the only place on earth.

Well, we agreed that night that we would meet here again exactly twenty years from that date and time, no matter what our conditions might be or from what distance we might have to come.

We figured that in twenty years each of us would know what kind of men we were, and what future waited for us and that we would make our fortunes."

SCENE 3

"It sounds pretty interesting," said the policeman.

"Rather a long time between meetings," it seems to me.

"Haven't you heard from your friend since you left?"

"Well, yes, for a time we corresponded," said the other.

"But after a year or two we lost track of each other.

You see, the West is pretty big, and I kept moving around

everywhere pretty quickly. But I know Jimmy will meet me here if he's alive, for he always was the truest, stanchest old chap in the world. He'll never forget.

I came a thousand miles to stand in this door tonight, and it's worth it if my old partner turns up."

The waiting man pulled out a handsome watch, the lids of it set with small diamonds.

"Three minutes to ten," he announced. "It was exactly ten o'clock when we parted here at the restaurant door."

"You were successful in the West, weren't you?" asked the policeman.

"I surely was! I hope Jimmy has done half as well. He was a kind of plodder, though, good fellow as he was. I've had to compete with some of the sharpest wits to make my fortune. A man gets in a groove in New York. In the West you learn how to fight for your success."

SCENE 4

The policeman twirled his club and took a step or two.

"I'll be on my way.

Hope your friend comes around all right.

Are you going to leave if he isn't here at ten sharp?"

"I should say not!" said the other.

"I'll give him half an hour at least.

If Jimmy is alive on earth he'll be here by that time.

So long, officer."

"Good-night, sir," said the policeman, passing on along his beat, trying doors as he went.

There was now a fine, cold drizzle falling, and the wind got stronger, so now it blew steadily.

The few pedestrians in that quarter hurried dismally and silently along with coat collars turned high and their hands in their pockets. And in the door of the hardware store, the man who had come a thousand miles to keep an appointment with the friend of his youth, smoked his cigar and waited. Such a meeting could be uncertain almost to absurdity.

About twenty minutes he waited, and then a tall man in a long overcoat, with collar turned up to his ears, hurried across from the opposite side of the street. He went directly to the waiting man.

SCENE 5

"Is that you, Bob?" he asked, doubtfully.

"Is that you, Jimmy Wells?" cried the man in the door.

The new arrival grasped both the other's hands with his own.

"It's Bob, sure as fate. I was certain I'd find you here if you were still in existence. Well, well, well! - twenty years is a long time. The old restaurant's gone, Bob; I wish it had lasted, so we could have had another dinner there. How has the West treated you, old man?"

"Incredible; it has given me everything I asked it for.

You've changed lots, Jimmy.

I never thought you were so tall."

"Oh, I grew a bit after I was twenty."

"Doing well in New York, Jimmy?"

"Moderately. I have a position in one of the city departments. Come on, Bob; we'll go around to a place I know of, and have a good long talk about old times." The two men started up the street, arm in arm.

The man from the West, his egotism enlarged by success, was beginning to tell the story of his career. The other, submerged in his overcoat, listened with interest.

At the corner stood a drug store, brilliant with electric lights. When they came into this glare each of them turned simultaneously to gaze upon the other's face.

SCENE 6

The man from the West stopped suddenly and released his arm.
"You're not Jimmy Wells," he snapped.
"Twenty years is a long time, but not long enough to change a man's nose from a Roman to a pug."
"It sometimes changes a good man into a bad one", said the tall man.
"You've been under arrest for ten minutes, Bob.
The Chicago cops thought you would come to New York.
They told us to watch for you.
They want to have a chat with you.
Are you coming with me quietly?
That's sensible.
Now, before we go on to the police station here's a note I was asked to hand to you. You may read it here at the window. It's from Patrolman Wells."
The man from the West unfolded the little piece of paper handed him. His hand was steady when he began to read, but it trembled a little by the time he had finished. The note was rather short.

"Bob: I was at the appointed place on time.
When you struck the match to light your cigar
I saw it was the face of the man wanted in Chicago.
Somehow I couldn't do it myself, so I went around
and got a plain clothes man to do the job.

JIMMY."

🍃 The Gift of the Magi 🍃

SCENE 1

One dollar and eighty-seven cents. That was all. And sixty cents of it was in pennies. Pennies saved one and two at a time by bulldozing the grocer and the vegetable man and the butcher until one's cheeks burned with the silent condemnation of being stingy that such close dealing accompanies. Three times Della counted it. One dollar and eighty-seven cents. And the next day would be Christmas.

There was clearly nothing to do but flop down on the shabby little couch and cry. So Della did it. That leads to the moral reflection that life is made up of sobs, sniffles, and smiles, with sniffles predominating.

While the mistress of the home is gradually subsiding from the first stage to the second, take a look at the home. A furnished flat at $8 per week. It was not exactly beyond description, but it certainly had to be on the lookout for a crowd of beggars.

In the hall below was a letter-box into which no letter would go, and an electric bell from which no mortal finger could ring. Also beside the door was a card bearing the name "Mr. James Dillingham Young."

SCENE 2

The "Dillingham" had been flung to the breeze during a former period of prosperity when its possessor was being paid $30 per week. Now, when the income was shrunk to $20, the letters of "Dillingham" looked blurred, as though they were thinking

seriously of contracting to a modest and unassuming D.
But whenever Mr. James Dillingham Young came home and reached his flat above he was called "Jim" and greatly hugged by Mrs. James Dillingham Young, already introduced to you as Della. That is all very good.

Della finished her cry and attended to her cheeks with the powder rag. She stood by the window and looked out dully at a grey cat walking a grey fence in a grey backyard.

Tomorrow would be Christmas Day, and she had only $1.87 with which to buy Jim a present. She had been saving every penny she could for months, with this result. Twenty dollars a week doesn't go far. Expenses had been greater than she had calculated. They always are. Only $1.87 to buy a present for Jim. Her Jim. Many a happy hour she had spent planning for something nice for him. Something fine and rare and excellent -something just a little bit near to being worthy of the honor of being owned by Jim.

SCENE 3

There was a pier-glass between the windows of the room. Perhaps you have seen a pier-glass in an $8 flat. A very thin and very agile person may, by observing his reflection in a rapid sequence of longitudinal strips, obtain a fairly accurate conception of his looks. Della, being slender, had mastered the art.

Suddenly she whirled from the window and stood before the glass. Her eyes were shining brilliantly, but her face had lost its color within twenty seconds. Rapidly she pulled down her hair and let it fall to its full length.

Now, there were two possessions of the James Dillingham Youngs in which they both took a mighty pride. One was Jim's gold watch that had been his father's and his grandfather's. The other was

Della's hair.

Had a queen lived in the flat near theirs, Della would have let her hair hang out the window some day to dry just to depreciate Her Majesty's jewels and gifts.

Had King Solomon been the janitor, with all his treasures piled up in the basement, Jim would have pulled out his watch every time he passed, just to see him pluck at his beard from envy.

SCENE 4

So now Della's beautiful hair fell about her, rippling and shining like a cascade of brown waters. It reached below her knee and made itself almost a garment for her. And then she did it up again nervously and quickly. Once she faltered for a minute and stood still while a tear or two splashed on the worn red carpet.

She put on her old brown jacket; she put on her old brown hat. With a whirl of skirts and with the brilliant sparkle still in her eyes, she fluttered out the door and down the stairs to the street. Where she stopped he sign read: "Mme. Sofronie. Hair Goods of All Kinds." One flight up Della ran, and collected herself, panting.

Madame, large, too white, chilly, hardly looked the "Sofronie."

"Will you buy my hair?" asked Della.

"I buy hair," said Madame.

"Take your hat off and let's have a sight at the looks of it."

Down rippled the brown cascade.

"Twenty dollars," said Madame, lifting the mass with a practiced hand.

"Give it to me quick," said Della.

Oh, and the next two hours tripped by on rosy wings.

Forget the hashed metaphor.

She was ransacking the stores for Jim's present.

SCENE 5

She found a gift for Jim at last. It surely had been made for Jim and no one else. There was no other like it in any of the stores, and she had looked in every store in the city. It was a gold watch chain simple and chaste in design, properly proclaiming its value by substance alone and not by flashy ornamentation -as all good things should do. It was even worthy of The Watch.

As soon as she saw it she knew that it must be Jim's. It was like him. Quietness and value - the description applied to both. Twenty-one dollars they took from her for it, and she hurried home with the 87 cents.

With that chain on his watch Jim could look at his watch and learn the time in any company. Grand as the watch was, he sometimes looked at it on the sly on account of the old leather strap that he used in place of a chain.

When Della reached home her intoxication gave way a little to prudence and reason. She got out her curling irons and lighted the gas and went to work repairing the ravages made by generosity added to love. That is always a tremendous task, dear friends -a mammoth task.

Within forty minutes her head was covered with tiny, close-lying curls that made her look wonderfully like a truant schoolboy. She looked at her reflection in the mirror long and carefully.

SCENE 6

"If Jim doesn't kill me," she said to herself, "before he takes a second look at me, he'll say I look like a Coney Island chorus girl. But what could I do -oh! what could I do with a dollar and eighty-seven cents?"

At 7 o'clock the coffee was made and the frying-pan was on the back of the stove hot and ready to cook the chops.

Jim was never late. Della doubled the watch chain in her hand and sat on the corner of the table near the door that he always entered. Then she heard his step on the stair away down on the first flight, and she turned white for just a moment. She had a habit for saying little silent prayers about the simplest everyday things, and now she whispered: "Please God, make him think I am still pretty."

The door opened and Jim stepped in and closed it.

He looked thin and very serious.

Poor fellow, he was only twenty-two - and to be burdened with a family!

He needed a new overcoat and he was without gloves.

Jim stopped inside the door, as immovable as a setter at the scent of quail. His eyes were fixed upon Della, and there was an expression in them that she could not read, and it terrified her. It was not anger, nor surprise, nor disapproval, nor horror, nor any of the sentiments that she had been prepared for. He simply stared at her fixedly with that peculiar expression on his face.

SCENE 7

Della wriggled off the table and went for him.

"Jim, darling," she cried, "don't look at me that way.

I had my hair cut off and sold it because I couldn't have lived through Christmas without giving you a present.

It'll grow out again - you won't mind, will you?

I just had to do it.

My hair grows awfully fast.

Say 'Merry Christmas!' Jim, and let's be happy.

You don't know what a nice - what a beautiful, nice gift I've got for you."

"You've cut off your hair?" asked Jim, slowly, as if he had not taken in that patent fact yet even after the hardest mental labor.

"Cut it off and sold it," said Della.

"Don't you like me just as well, anyhow?

I'm me without my hair, ain't I?"

Jim looked about the room curiously.

"You say your hair is gone?" he said, with an air almost of idiocy.

"You needn't look for it," said Della.

"It's sold, I tell you - sold and gone, too.

It's Christmas Eve, boy.

Be good to me, for it went for you.

Maybe the hairs of my head were numbered," she went on with sudden serious sweetness, "but nobody could ever count my love for you.

Shall I put the chops on, Jim?"

SCENE 8

Out of his trance Jim seemed quickly to wake. He enfolded his Della. For ten seconds let us regard with discreet scrutiny some inconsequential object in the other direction. Eight dollars a week or a million a year -what is the difference? A mathematician or a wit would give you the wrong answer. The magi brought valuable gifts, but that was not among them. This dark assertion will be illuminated later on.

Jim drew a package from his overcoat pocket and threw it upon the table. "Don't make any mistake, Dell," he said, "about me.

I don't think there's anything in the way of a haircut or a shave or a shampoo that could make me like my girl any less.

But if you'll unwrap that package you may see what I felt a while at first."

White fingers tore at the string and paper.

And then an ecstatic scream of joy; and then, alas! a quick feminine change to hysterical tears and wails, necessitating the immediate employment of all the comforting powers of the lord of the flat. For there lay The Combs - the set of combs, side and back, that Della had seen in a Broadway window and loved for long. Beautiful combs, pure tortoise shell, with jewelled rims, perfect for the beautiful hair. They were expensive combs, she knew, and her heart had simply craved and yearned over them without the least hope of possession. And now, they were hers, but the tresses that should have adorned the coveted adornments were gone.

SCENE 9

But she hugged them to her bosom, and at length she was able to look up with dim eyes and a smile and say: "My hair grows so fast, Jim!"

And then Della leaped up like a little singed cat and cried, "Oh, oh!"

Jim had not yet seen his beautiful present.

She held it out to him eagerly upon her open palm.

The precious metal seemed to flash with a reflection of her bright and ardent spirit.

"Isn't it dandy, Jim?

I hunted all over the town to find it.

You'll have to look at the time a hundred times a day now.

Give me your watch.

I want to see how it looks on it."

Instead of obeying, Jim flopped down on the couch and put his hands under the back of his head and smiled.

"Dell," said he, "let's put our Christmas presents away and keep them a while. They're too nice to use just at present.
I sold the watch to get the money to buy your combs.
And now I suppose we should have dinner."

SCENE 10

The magi, as you know, were wise men -wonderfully wise men -who brought gifts to the Babe in the manger. They invented the custom of giving Christmas presents. Being wise, their gifts were no doubt wise ones, possibly bearing the privilege of exchange in case of duplication. And here I have lamely related to you the uneventful narrative of two foolish children in a flat who most unwisely sacrificed for each other the greatest treasures of their house. But let me speak a last word to the wise of these days of all who give gifts these two were the wisest.
Of all who give and receive gifts, such as they are wisest.
Everywhere they are wisest.
They are the magi.

🍂 Two Thanksgiving Day Gentlemen 🍂

SCENE 1

There is one day that is ours. There is one day when all we Americans who are not self-made go back to the old home to eat a big dinner and marvel how much nearer to the porch the old pump looks than it used to. Bless the day. President Roosevelt gives it to us. Sometimes he talks about the Puritans who had the first Thanksgiving. But we don't just remember who they were. They were some people who landed on Plymouth Rocks. Well, that sounds more familiar. Lots of us have had to come down to hens since the Turkey Trust was formed. The big city east of the cranberry bogs has made Thanksgiving Day an institution. The last Thursday in November is the only day in the year on which we have turkey for Thanksgiving dinner. It is the one day that is purely American. Yes, a day of celebration, exclusively American.
And now the story is to prove to you that we have traditions on this side of the ocean that are getting older at a much more rapid rate than those of England are -thanks to our git-up and enterprise. Stuffy Pete took his seat on the third bench to the right as you enter Union Square from the east, at the walk opposite the fountain. Every Thanksgiving Day for nine years he had taken his seat there promptly at 1 o'clock. Every time, things had happened to him -Charles Dickensy things that swelled his waistcoat above his heart, and equally on the other side.

SCENE 2

But today Stuffy Pete's appearance at the annual trysting place seemed to have been rather the result of habit than of the yearly hunger which, as the philanthropists seem to think, afflicts the poor only on Thanksgiving Day.

Certainly Pete was not hungry. He had just come from a feast that had left him of his powers barely those of respiration and locomotion. His eyes were like two pale gooseberries firmly imbedded in a swollen and gravy-smeared mask of putty. His breath came in short wheezes; a senatorial roll of fat tissue denied a fashionable set to his upturned coat collar. Buttons that had been sewed upon his clothes by kind Salvation fingers a week before flew like popcorn; strewing the earth around him. Ragged he was, with a split shirt front open to the wishbone; but the November breeze, carrying fine snowflakes, brought him only a grateful coolness. For Stuffy Pete was overheated with the caloric produced by a bountiful dinner, beginning with oysters and ending with plum pudding, and including (it seemed to him) all the roast turkey and baked potatoes and chicken salad and squash pie and ice cream in the world. So he sat, gorged, and gazed upon the world with after-dinner contempt. The meal had been an unexpected one. He was passing a red brick mansion near the beginning of Fifth avenue, in which lived two old ladies of ancient family and a reverence for traditions. They even denied the existence of New York, and believed that Thanksgiving Day was declared solely for Washington Square.

SCENE 3

One of their traditional habits was to station a servant at the back gate with orders to admit the first hungry traveler that walked by after the hour of noon had struck, and banquet him until he could eat his fill. Stuffy Pete happened to pass by on his way to the park, and the servants gathered him in and upheld the custom of the castle.

After Stuffy Pete had gazed straight before him for ten minutes he felt a desire to look in another direction. With a tremendous effort he moved his head slowly to the left. And then his eyes bulged out fearfully, and his breath ceased, and his feet in their torn shoes at the ends of his short legs wriggled and rustled on the gravel. For the Old Gentleman was coming across Fourth avenue toward his bench. Every Thanksgiving Day for nine years the Old Gentleman had come there and found Stuffy Pete on his bench. That was a thing that the Old Gentleman was trying to make a tradition of. Every Thanksgiving Day for nine years he had found Stuffy there, and had led him to a restaurant and watched him eat a big dinner. They do those things in England unconsciously. But this is a young country, and nine years is not so bad. The Old Gentleman was a staunch American patriot, and considered himself a pioneer in American tradition. In order to become picturesque we must keep on doing one thing for a long time without ever letting it get away from us. Something like collecting the weekly dimes in industrial insurance. Or cleaning the streets.

SCENE 4

The Old Gentleman moved, straight and stately, toward the Institution that he was rearing. Truly, feeding Stuffy Pete once a year was nothing national in its character, such as the Magna Charta or jam for breakfast was in England. But it was a step. It was almost feudal. It showed, at least, that a Custom was not impossible to New Y-ahem!-America.

The Old Gentleman was thin and tall and sixty. He was dressed all in black, and wore the old-fashioned kind of glasses that won't stay on your nose. His hair was whiter and thinner than it had been last year, and he seemed to make more use of his big, knobby cane with the crooked handle.

As his established benefactor came up Stuffy wheezed and shuddered like some woman's over-fat pug when a street dog bristles up at him. He would have flown, but he could not move from his bench. Well had the servants of the two old ladies done their work.

"Good morning," said the Old Gentleman.

"I am glad to perceive that the vicissitudes of another year have spared you to move in health about the beautiful world. Thanks to that blessing, you and I could meet on this day of thanksgiving. If you will come with me, my man, I will provide you with a dinner that should make your physical being accord with the mental."

SCENE 5

That is what the old Gentleman said every time. Every Thanksgiving Day for nine years. The words themselves almost formed an Institution. Nothing could be compared with them except the Declaration of Independence. Always before, they had been music in Stuffy's ears. But now he looked up at the Old Gentleman's face with tearful agony in his own. The fine snow turned quickly to water when it fell upon his perspiring brow. But the Old Gentleman shivered a little and turned his back to the wind.

Stuffy had always wondered why the Old Gentleman looked sad as he spoke. He did not know that it was because he was wishing every time that he had a son to succeed him. A son who would come there after he was gone -a son who would stand proud and strong before some subsequent Stuffy, and say: "In memory of my father." Then it would be an Institution.

But the Old Gentleman had no relatives. He lived in rented rooms in one of the decayed old family brownstone mansions in one of the quiet streets east of the park. In the winter he raised a few flowers in a little conservatory the size of a trunk. In the spring he walked in the Easter parade. In the summer he lived at a farmhouse in the New Jersey hills, and sat in a wicker armchair, speaking of a strange butterfly, that he hoped to find some day. In the autumn he fed Stuffy a dinner. These were the Old Gentleman's occupations.

SCENE 6

Stuffy Pete looked up at the Old Gentleman for a half minute, stewing and helpless in his own self-pity. The Old Gentleman's eyes were bright with the giving-pleasure. His face was getting more lined each year, but his little black necktie was in as jaunty a bow as ever, and his clothes were beautiful and white, and his gray mustache was curled at the ends. And then Stuffy made a noise that sounded like peas bubbling in a pot.

He intended to speak; and as the Old Gentleman had heard the sounds nine times before, he rightly construed them into Stuffy's old way of acceptance.

"Thank you, sir. I'll go with you, and much obliged. I'm very hungry, sir."

The coma of repletion had not prevented from entering Stuffy's mind the conviction that he was the basis of an Institution. His Thanksgiving appetite was not his own; it belonged to this kind old gentleman by all the sacred rights of established custom, since the Old Gentleman had preempted it.

True, America is free; but in order to establish tradition some one must follow it every year. The heroes are not all heroes of steel and gold. See one here that wielded only weapons of iron, badly silvered, and tin.

The Old Gentleman led his annual protege southward to the restaurant, and to the table where the feast had always occurred. They were known at this place.

SCENE 7

"Here comes the old guy," said a waiter, "the man buy the same bum a meal every Thanksgiving."

The Old Gentleman sat across the table glowing like a pearl at his corner-stone of future ancient Tradition. The waiters heaped the table with holiday food -and Stuffy, with a sigh that was mistaken for hunger's expression, raised knife and fork and carved the meat into thin slices.

No hero ever fought valiantly against an enemy. Turkey, chops, soups, vegetables, pies, disappeared before him as fast as they could be served. Gorged nearly to the uttermost when he entered the restaurant, the smell of food had almost caused him to lose his honor as a gentleman, but he rallied like a true knight. He saw the look of beneficent happiness on the Old Gentleman's face -a happier look than even a flower or a strange butterfly had ever brought to it -and he had not the heart to see it wane.

In an hour Stuffy leaned back with a battle won. "Thank you, sir," he puffed like a leaky steam pipe; "thank you for a hearty meal." Then he arose heavily with glazed eyes and started toward the kitchen. A waiter turned him about like a top, and pointed him toward the door. The Old Gentleman carefully counted out $1.30 in silver change, leaving three nickels for the waiter.

They parted as they did each year at the door, the Old Gentleman going south, Stuffy north.

SCENE 8

Around the first corner Stuffy turned, and stood for one minute. Then he fell to the sidewalk like a sunstricken horse.

When the ambulance came the young surgeon and the driver cursed softly at his weight. There was no smell of whiskey to justify a transfer to the patrol wagon, so Stuffy and his two dinners went to the hospital. There they stretched him on a bed and began to test him for strange diseases, with the hope of getting a chance at some problem with the scalpel.

And lo! an hour later another ambulance brought the Old Gentleman. And they laid him on another bed and spoke of appendicitis, for he looked good for the bill.

But pretty soon one of the young doctors met one of the young nurses whose eyes he liked, and stopped to chat with her about the cases.

"That nice old gentleman over there, now," he said, "you wouldn't think that was a case of almost starvation.

Proud old family, I guess.

He told me he hadn't eaten a thing for three days."

🍃 A Retrieved Reformation 🍃

SCENE 1

A guard came to the prison shoe-shop, where Jimmy Valentine was assiduously stitching uppers, and escorted him to the prison office. There the warden handed Jimmy his pardon, which had been signed that morning by the governor. Jimmy took it in a tired kind of way. He had served nearly ten months of a four year sentence. He had expected to stay only about three months, at the longest. Jimmy Valentine had many influential friends outside the prison. It is hardly worth his while to cut his hair.

"Now, Valentine," said the warden, "you'll go out in the morning. Brace up, and make a man of yourself.

You're not a bad fellow at heart. Stop cracking safes, and live straight."

"Me?" said Jimmy, in surprise.

"Why, I never cracked a safe in my life."

"Oh, no," laughed the warden.

"Of course not. Let's see, now.

How was it you happened to get sent to prison on that Springfield job?

Was it because you wouldn't prove an alibi for fear of compromising somebody in high society?

Or was it simply a case of a mean old jury that had it in for you? You men always have a reason like that.

You never went to prison if you didn't crack a safe."

"Me?" said Jimmy, still blankly innocent.

"Why, warden, I never was in Springfield in my life!"

"Take him back, Cronin!" said the warden, "and give him outgoing clothes.

Unlock him at seven in the morning, and let him come to the bull-pen.

Better think over my advice, Valentine."

SCENE 2

At a quarter past seven on the next morning Jimmy stood in the warden's outer office. He had on a suit of the non-matching, ready-made clothes and a pair of the stiff, squeaky shoes that the state furnishes to its discharged compulsory guests.

The clerk handed him a railroad ticket and the five-dollar bill with which the law expected him to rehabilitate himself into good citizenship and prosperity. The warden gave him a cigar, and shook hands. Valentine, 9762, was chronicled on the books, "Pardoned by Governor," and Mr. James Valentine walked out into the sunshine. Disregarding the song of the birds, the waving green trees, and the smell of the flowers, Jimmy headed straight for a restaurant. There he tasted the first sweet joys of liberty in the shape of a broiled chicken and a bottle of white wine-followed by a cigar a grade better than the one the warden had given him. From there he proceeded leisurely to the depot. He tossed a quarter into the hat of a blind man sitting by the door, and boarded his train. Three hours set him down in a little town near the state line. He went to the cafe of Mike Dolan and shook hands with Mike, who was alone behind the bar.

SCENE 3

"Sorry we couldn't do it sooner, Jimmy, my boy," said Mike. "But we had that protest from Springfield to buck against, and the governor nearly balked. Feeling all right?"

"Fine," said Jimmy. "Got my key?"

He got his key and went upstairs, unlocking the door of a room at the rear. Everything was just as he had left it. There on the floor was still Ben Price's collar-button that had been torn from that eminent detective's coat when they had overpowered Jimmy to arrest him. Pulling out from the wall a folding-bed, Jimmy slid back a panel in the wall and dragged out a dust-covered suit-case. He opened this and gazed fondly at the finest set of burglar's tools in the East. It was a complete set, made of specially tempered steel in various shapes and sizes, invented by Jimmy himself, in which he took pride. Over nine hundred dollars they had cost him to have made at a place where they make such things for the safebreaking profession.

In half an hour Jimmy went down stairs and through the cafe. He was now dressed in tasteful and well-fitting clothes, and carried his dusted and cleaned suit-case in his hand.

SCENE 4

"Do you have anything on?" asked Mike Dolan, genially.

"Me?" said Jimmy, in a puzzled tone.

"I don't understand.

I work for the New York Biscuit Cracker and cake Company.

And I sell the best cracker and cake in the country."

This statement delighted Mike to such an extent that Jimmy had to take a drink with him on the spot. He never touched "hard" drinks. A week after the release of Valentine, 9762, there was a neat job of safe-burglary done in Richmond, Indiana, with no clue who did it. A scant eight hundred dollars was taken. Two weeks after that a patented, improved, burglar-proof safe in Logansport was opened like a cheese. Fifteen hundred dollars in cash were taken, securities and silver untouched. That began to interest the detectives. Then an old-fashioned bank-safe in Jefferson City was opened and bank-notes amounting to five thousand dollars were taken. The losses were now high enough to bring the matter up into Ben Price's class of work. By comparing notes, a remarkable similarity in the methods of the burglaries was noticed. Ben Price investigated the scenes of the robberies, and was heard to remark: "That's Dandy Jim Valentine's autograph. He's resumed business.

Look at that combination knob -jerked out as easy as pulling up a radish in wet weather. Only he's got the tools that can do it.

And look how clean those tumblers were punched out!

Jimmy never has to drill but one hole. Yes, I want Mr. Valentine. He'll do his bit next time without any short-time or clemency foolishness."

SCENE 5

Ben Price knew Jimmy's habits. He had learned them while working on the Springfield case. Long escapes, quick get-aways, no accomplices, and a taste for good society -these ways had helped Mr. Valentine to become noted as a successful dodger of retribution. It was widely known that Ben Price had taken up the trail of the elusive cracksman, and other people with burglar-proof safes felt more at ease.

One afternoon Jimmy Valentine and his suit-case climbed out of the mail coach in Elmore, a small town, Arkansas. Jimmy, looking like an athletic senior just home from college, went down the board side-walk toward the hotel.

A young lady crossed the street, passed him at the corner and entered a door over which was the sign, "The Elmore Bank." Jimmy

Valentine looked into her eyes, forgot what he was, and became another man. She lowered her eyes and had red cheeks. Young men of Jimmy's style and looks were scarce in Elmore.

Jimmy collared a boy that was loafing on the steps of the bank as if he were one of the stockholders, and began to ask him questions about the town, handing him dimes at intervals. By and by the young lady came out, looking unconscious of the young man with the suit-case, and went her way.

"Isn't that young lady Polly Simpson?" asked Jimmy, with specious guile.

SCENE 6

"No," said the boy. "She's Annabel Adams. Her father owns this bank.

What did you come to Elmore for?

Is that a gold watch-chain?

I'm going to get a bulldog. Got any more dimes?"

Jimmy went to the Planters' Hotel, registered as Ralph D. Spencer, and engaged a room. He leaned on the desk and and he told the clerk he had come to Elmore to look for a location to go into business.

How was the shoe business, now, in the town?

He had thought of the shoe business.

Was there already a shoe-shop?

The clerk was impressed by the clothes and manner of Jimmy. He was something of a pattern of fashion to the youth of Elmore, but he now perceived his shortcomings. While trying to figure out Jimmy's manner of tying his four-in-hand, he cordially gave information.

Yes, there must be a good opening in the shoe line.

There wasn't an exclusive shoe-store in the place.
The dry-goods and general stores handled them.
Business in all lines was fairly good.
He hoped Mr. Spencer would decide to stay in Elmore.
He would find it a pleasant town to live in, and the people very sociable.
Mr. Spencer thought he would stop over in the town a few days and look over the situation. No, the clerk needn't call the boy. He would carry up his suit-case, himself; it was rather heavy. Mr. Ralph Spencer, the phoenix that arose from Jimmy Valentine's ashes -ashes left by the flame of a sudden and alternative attack of love -remained in Elmore, and prospered. He opened a shoe-store and business was good.

SCENE 7

Socially he was also a success, and made many friends. And he accomplished the wish of his heart. He met Miss Annabel Adams, and became more and more captivated by her charms.
At the end of a year the situation of Mr. Ralph Spencer was this: he had won the respect of the community, his shoe-store was flourishing, and he and Annabel were engaged to be married in two weeks. Mr. Adams, the typical, plodding, country banker, approved of Spencer. Annabel's pride in him almost equalled her affection. He was as much at home in the family of Mr. Adams and that of Annabel's married sister as if he were already a member.
One day Jimmy sat down in his room and wrote this letter, which he mailed to the safe address of one of his old friends in St. Louis:

Dear Old Pal:
I want you to be at Sullivan's place, in Little Rock, next Wednesday

night, at nine o'clock. I want you to wind up some little matters for me. And, also, I want to make you a present of my kit of tools. I know you'll be glad to get them -you couldn't duplicate them for a thousand dollars. Say, Billy, I've quit the old business-a year ago. I've got a nice store. I'm making an honest living, and I'm going to marry the finest girl on earth two weeks from now. It's the only life, Billy -the straight one. I wouldn't touch a dollar of another man's money now for a million. After I get married I'm going to sell out and go West, where there won't be so much danger of seeing anyone who knew me in my old life. I tell you, Billy, she's an angel. She believes in me; and I wouldn't do another crooked thing for the whole world. Be sure to be at Sully's, for I must see you. I'll bring along the tools with me.

Your old friend,
Jimmy.

SCENE 8

On the Monday night after Jimmy wrote this letter, Ben Price jogged quietly into Elmore in a buggy. He lounged about town in his quiet way until he found out what he wanted to know. From the drug-store across the street from Spencer's shoe-store he got a good look at Ralph D. Spencer.

"Going to marry the banker's daughter are you, Jimmy?" said Ben to himself.

"Well, I don't know!"

The next morning Jimmy took breakfast at the Adamses. He was going to Little Rock that day to order his wedding-suit and buy something nice for Annabel. That would be the first time he had left town since he came to Elmore. It had been more than a year now since those last professional "jobs," and he thought he could safely venture out.

After breakfast most of the Adams family went downtown together -Mr. Adams, Annabel, Jimmy, and Annabel's married sister with her two little girls, aged five and nine. They came by the hotel where Jimmy still boarded, and he ran up to his room and brought along his suit-case. Then they went on to the bank. There stood Jimmy's horse and buggy and Dolph Gibson, who was going to drive him over to the railroad station.

All went inside the high, carved oak railings into the banking-room -Jimmy included, for Mr. Adams's future son-in-law was welcome anywhere. The clerks were pleased to be greeted by the good-looking, agreeable young man who was going to marry Miss Annabel. Jimmy set his suit-case down. Annabel, whose heart was bubbling with happiness and lively youth, put on Jimmy's hat, and picked up the suit-case.

"Wouldn't I make a nice salesperson?" said Annabel.

"My! Ralph, how heavy it is? Feels like it was full of gold bricks."

SCENE 9

"Lot of nickel-plated shoe-horns in there," said Jimmy, coolly, "that I'm going to return. Thought I'd save express charges by taking them up. I'm getting awfully economical."

The Elmore Bank had just put in a new safe. Mr. Adams was very proud of it, and insisted on an inspection by every one. The vault was a small one, but it had a new, patented door. It fastened with three solid steel bolts with a single handle, and had a time-lock. Mr. Adams beamingly explained its workings to Mr. Spencer, who showed a courteous interest but not too intelligent one. The two children, May and Agatha, were delighted by the shining metal and funny lock and knobs.

While they were thus engaged Ben Price sauntered in and leaned on his elbow, looking casually inside between the railings. He told the teller that he didn't want anything; he was just waiting for a man he knew.

Suddenly there was a scream or two from the women, and a commotion. Unperceived by the elders, May, the nine-year-old girl, in a spirit of play, had shut Agatha in the vault. She had then closed the door of the safe and turned the knob of the combination as she had seen Mr. Adams do.

The old banker sprang to the handle and tugged at it for a moment. "The door can't be opened," he groaned.

"The clock hasn't been wound nor the combination set."

Agatha's mother screamed again, hysterically.

SCENE 10

"Hush!" said Mr. Adams, raising his trembling hand.

"All be quite for a moment. Agatha!" he called as loudly as he could.

"Listen to me."

During the following silence they could just hear the faint sound of the child wildly shrieking in the dark vault in a panic of terror.

"My precious darling!" wailed the mother.

"She will die of fright! Open the door! Oh, break it open! Can't you men do something?"

"There isn't a man nearer than Little Rock who can open that door," said Mr. Adams, in a shaky voice.

"My God! Spencer, what shall we do?

That child-she can't stand it long in there.

There isn't enough air, and, besides, she'll go into convulsions from fright."

Agatha's mother, frantic now, beat the door of the vault with her hands. Somebody wildly suggested dynamite. Annabel turned to Jimmy, her large eyes full of anguish, but not yet despairing. To a woman nothing seems quite impossible to the powers of the man she worships. "Can't you do something, Ralph?"

He looked at her with a queer, soft smile on his lips and in his keen eyes. "Annabel," he said, "give me that rose you are wearing, will you?"

Hardly believing that she heard him rightly, she unpinned the bud from the bosom of her dress, and placed it in his hand. Jimmy stuffed it into his vest-pocket, threw off his coat and pulled up his shirt-sleeves. With that act Ralph D. Spencer passed away and Jimmy Valentine took his place. "Get away from the door, all of you," he commanded, shortly.

SCENE 11

He set his suit-case on the table, and opened it out flat. From that time on he seemed to be unconscious of the presence of any one else. He laid out the shining, queer implements swiftly and orderly, whistling softly to himself as he always did when at work. In a deep silence and immovable, the others watched him as if under a spell. In a minute Jimmy's pet drill was biting smoothly into the steel door. In ten minutes —breaking his own burglarious record —he threw back the bolts and opened the door.

Agatha, almost collapsed, but safe, was gathered into her mother's arms.

Jimmy Valentine put on his coat, and walked outside the railings towards the front door. As he went he thought he heard a far-away voice that called him "Ralph!" He once knew it but he never hesitated.

At the door a big man stood in his way.

"Hello, Ben!" said Jimmy, still with his strange smile.

"You're here at last, aren't you?

Well, let's go.

I know that it makes no difference, now."

And then Ben Price acted rather strangely.

"Guess you're mistaken, Mr. Spencer," he said.

"Don't believe I recognize you.

Your buggy's waiting for you, ain't it?"

And Ben Price turned and strolled down the street.

🍃 The Cop and the Anthem 🍃

SCENE 1

On his bench in Madison Square Soapy moved uneasily. When wild geese begin to fly south, and when women without sealskin coats grow kind to their husbands, and when Soapy moves uneasily on his bench in the park, you may know that winter is near at hand. A dead leaf fell in Soapy's lap. That was Jack Frost's calling card. Jack is kind to the inhabitants of Madison Square, and warns them of his annual call. At the corners of four streets, he hands his calling cards to the North Wind, so that the inhabitants may make ready for the coming winter.

Soapy realized the fact that the time had come for him to find ways to provide against the coming winter. And therefore he moved uneasily on his park bench.

Soapy did not have very high hopes for the winter. In them there were no considerations of cruising on a ship in the Mediterranean, of sailing away on a ship in the Bay of Naples. Three months in the prison on the Blackwell's Island was what he craved. Three months of assured board and bed and congenial company, safe from the cold north wind and cops, seemed to Soapy the most desirable thing in the world.

For years the prison on the Island had been his winter quarters. While his more fortunate fellow New Yorkers had bought their tickets to Palm Beach each winter, Soapy had made his humble arrangements to move into Blackwell Prison.

SCENE 2

And now the time had come. On the previous night three Sunday newspapers, some beneath his coat, some over his lap, had failed to repulse the cold as he slept on his bench near the spurting fountain in the ancient square. So the Island loomed big and timely in Soapy's mind. He scorned the provisions made in the name of charity for the city's dependents.

In Soapy's opinion the Law was more benign than Philanthropy. There were many charitable institutions, both municipal and religious, on which he might receive lodging and food accordant with the simple life. But to Soapy's proud spirit the gifts of charity are burdensome. If not in coin you must pay in humiliation of spirit for every benefit received at the hands of philanthropy. Whenever he got something for free, his pride was hurt. Every bed of charity must have its toll of a bath, every loaf of bread its price of a private and personal questions. So it is better to be a guest of the law, which though conducted by rules, does not meddle unduly with a gentleman's private affairs.

Soapy, having decided to go to the Island, at once set about accomplishing his desire. There were many easy ways of doing this. The most pleasant was to dine luxuriously at some expensive restaurant; and then, after declaring that he could not pay, be handed over quietly and without uproar to a policeman. An accommodating judge would do the rest.

SCENE 3

Soapy who had decided what to do left his bench and strolled out of the square and across the level sea of asphalt, where Broadway and Fifth Avenue flow together. Up Broadway he turned, and halted at a glittering cafe, where the choicest products of the grape are served, and the best people in the best clothes appear every night.

Soapy had confidence in his appearance from the lowest button of his vest upward. His face was shaven, and his coat was decent and his neat black tie had been presented to him by a lady missionary on Thanksgiving Day. If he could reach a table in the restaurant unsuspected success would be his. The part of him that would show above the table would raise no doubt in the waiter's mind. A roasted duck, thought Soapy, would be about the thing -with a bottle of wine, and then Camembert, a cup of strong coffee and a cigar. One dollar for the cigar would be enough. The total would not be so high as to demand an act of revenge from the cafe management; and yet the meat would leave him filled and happy for the journey to his winter refuge.

But as Soapy set foot inside the restaurant door the head waiter saw his frayed trousers and ruined shoes. Strong hands of several waiters turned him about and conveyed him in silence and haste to the sidewalk. So he missed the chance to have the roasted duck.

SCENE 4

Soapy turned off Broadway. It seemed that his route to the coveted island was not to be an epicurean one. He must think of some other way of getting to his winter haven.

At a corner of Sixth Avenue electric lights and cunningly displayed wares behind plate-glass made a shop window conspicuous. Soapy picked up a stone and threw it through the glass. People came running around the corner, a policeman in the lead. Soapy stood still, with his hands in his pockets, and smiled at the sight of the cop.

"Where's the man that done that?" inquired the officer excitedly.
"Don't you figure out that I might have had something to do with it?" said Soapy, not without sarcasm, but friendly, as one greets good fortune.

The policeman's mind refused to accept Soapy as a suspect. Men who smash windows do not remain there to talk to cops. They take to their heels. The policeman saw a man half way down the block running to catch a car. With drawn club he joined in the pursuit. Soapy, sick at heart, loafed along, twice unsuccessful.

On the opposite side of the street was another restaurant. It catered to customers with large appetites who were not rich. Its plates and atmosphere were thick; its soup and tablecloths thin. Into this place Soapy took his old shoes and torn trousers without challenge. At a table he sat and consumed beefsteak, pancakes, doughnuts and pie. And then to the waiter he revealed the fact that the minutest coin and himself were strangers.

SCENE 5

"Now, get busy and call a cop," said Soapy.

"And don't keep a gentleman waiting."

"No cop for you," said the waiter, with a voice like butter cakes and an eye like the cherry in a Manhattan cocktail.

"Hey, Con!"

The two waiters pitched Soapy upon his left ear on the callous pavement. He arose, joint by joint, as a carpenter's rule opens, and beat the dust from his clothes. Arrest seemed but a rosy dream. The Island seemed very far away. A policeman who stood before a drug store two doors away laughed and walked down the street.

Five blocks Soapy travelled before he gained the courage to try again. This time the opportunity presented what he described as a "cinch." A nice-looking young woman was standing before a show window gazing with great interest at its display of shaving mugs and ink-stands, and two yards from the window a large policeman with severe expression leaned against a water plug.

It was Soapy's plan to bother the young lady and be arrested on a charge of harassment. The combination of the refined and elegant appearance of his victim and the conscientious cop encouraged him to believe that he would soon feel the pleasant cop's hand upon his arm that would insure his winter quarters on the Island.

SCENE 6

Soapy straightened the lady missionary's ready-made tie and wore his hat tilted to one side. And he walked toward the young woman. He made eyes at her, cleared his throat loudly, smiled, smirked and made the offensive and ill-mannered remarks of the "womanizer." Out of the corner of his eye, Soapy saw that the policeman was watching him fixedly. The young woman moved away a few steps, and again kept looking at the shaving mugs on display. Soapy, boldly stepping to her side, raised his hat and said: "Ah there, Bedelia! Don't you want to come and play with me?"

The policeman was still looking. The persecuted young woman had only to beckon a finger to call the cop over, and Soapy would be on his way to his insular haven. Already he imagined he could feel the cozy warmth of the station-house. The young woman faced him and, stretching out a hand, caught Soapy's coat sleeve.

"Sure, Mike," she said joyfully, "if you'll blow me to a few drinks. I would have spoken to you sooner, but the cop was watching."

With the young woman holding his arm as ivy clings to his oak

Soapy walked past the policeman overcome with gloom.
He seemed doomed to liberty.
At the next corner he shook off his companion and ran. He halted in a district where streets are lighter, and people are more lively at night. Women in furs and men in great coats moved gaily in the wintry air.

SCENE 7

A sudden fear seized Soapy. He wondered if some dreadful enchantment had made him immune to arrest. The thought brought him a little of panic. When he came upon another policeman lounging grandly in front of a luminous theater he caught at the straw of "disorderly conduct."
On the sidewalk, Soapy began to yell drunken gibberish at the top of his voice. He danced, howled, raved and disturbed the passers-by. The policeman twirled his club, turned his back to Soapy and remarked to a citizen.
"He must be one of those Yale boys celebrating their victory over Hartford College in football. Noisy; but no harm. We've instructions to leave them shout."
Hopelessly, Soapy ceased his unavailing racket. Would never a policeman lay hands on him? In his fancy the Island seemed an unattainable paradise. He buttoned his thin coat against the chilling wind.
In a cigar store he saw a well-dressed man lighting a cigar. His silk umbrella he had set by the door on entering. Soapy stepped inside, took the umbrella and sauntered off with it slowly. The well-dressed man followed him quickly. "My umbrella," he said, sternly.
"Oh, is it?" sneered Soapy, adding insult to petit larceny.

"Well, why don't you call a policeman? I took it.
Your umbrella! Why don't you call a cop?
There stands one on the corner."

The umbrella owner slowed his steps. Soapy did likewise, with a presentiment that luck would again run against him. The policeman looked at the two curiously.

"Of course," said the umbrella man, "that is-well, you know how these mistakes occur. If it's your umbrella, I hope you'll excuse me. I picked it up this morning in a restaurant. If you recognize it as yours, I hope you'll-"

"Of course it's mine," said Soapy, viciously.

SCENE 8

The ex-umbrella man retreated. The policeman hurried to assist a tall blonde in a long coat across the street in front of a street car that was approaching two blocks away.

Soapy walked eastward through a street under construction. He hurled the umbrella wrathfully into an open hole. He muttered against the men who wear helmets and carry clubs. Because he wanted to fall into their hands, they seemed to regard him as a king who could do no wrong.

At length Soapy reached one of the avenues to the east where lights shone faintly and it was far quieter. He walked south toward Madison Square, for the homing instinct survived even though the home was a park bench.

But on an unusually quiet corner Soapy came to a standstill. Here was an old church, quaint and gabled. Through one violet-stained window a soft light glowed, where, no doubt, an organist was making soft music to practice for the coming Sunday anthem.

Sweet music came to Soapy's ears. It caught him transfixed against the iron fence.

The moon was above, lustrous and serene; vehicles and pedestrians were few; sparrows twittered sleepily in the eaves -for a little while the scene might have been a country churchyard. And the anthem that the organist played cemented Soapy to the iron fence, for he had known it well in the younger days. In those days his life contained such things as mothers and roses and ambitions and friends and immaculate thoughts and collars.

The conjunction of Soapy's receptive state of mind and the influences about the old church made a sudden and wonderful change in his soul. To his horror, he saw the bottomless pit of the hell into which he had tumbled. He realized that his life was full of the degraded days, unworthy desires, dead hopes, wrecked faculties and base motives.

SCENE 9

And also in a moment his heart responded thrillingly to this novel mood. An instantaneous and strong impulse moved him to battle with his desperate fate.

He would pull himself out of the mire; he would make a man of himself again; he would conquer the evil that had taken possession of him. There was time. He was comparatively young yet. He would resurrect his old eager ambitions and pursue them without faltering. Those solemn but sweet organ notes had set up a revolution in him. Tomorrow he would go into the roaring downtown district and find work. A fur importer had once offered him a place as a driver. He would find him tomorrow and ask for the position. He would be somebody in the world. He would---

Soapy felt a hand laid on his arm.

He looked quickly around into the face of a policeman.

"What are you doing here?" asked the officer.

"Nothing," said Soapy.

"Then come along," said the policeman.

"Three months on the Island," said the judge in the Police Court the next morning.